THE SEC OF PADEL

A guide to improve your level

Initiation (I) Initiation (II) Intermediate Advanced Professional

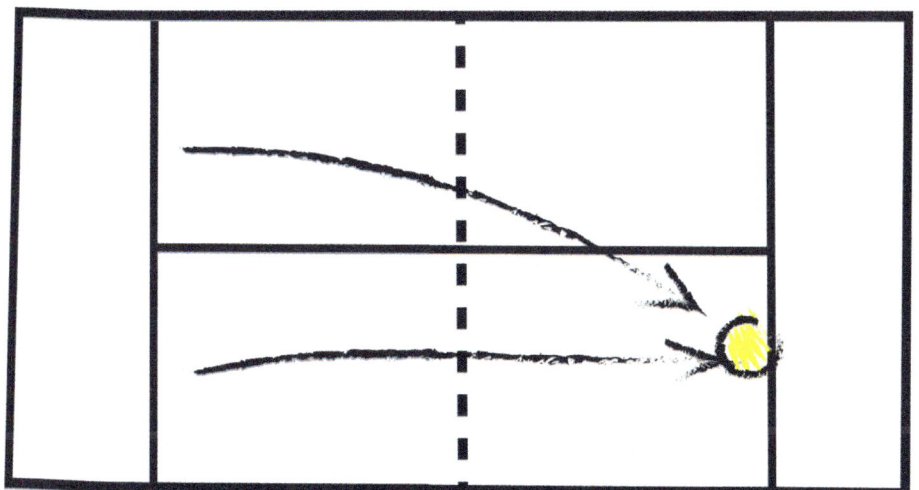

Ferran Insa Sotillo

ABOUT THE AUTHOR

Ferran Insa Sotillo was born in Granollers (Barcelona, Spain) in 1994. Passionate about sport and strategy. Footballer from the age of five to seventeen. Due to an injury, at the age of eighteen (2012) he started playing padel and three years later he played his first match in the World Padel Tour.

- Currently, World Padel Tour player.

- Graduated in Business Administration and Management from University of Barcelona (2018).

- Graduated in Law from University of Barcelona (2019).

- Best absolut university sportsman in Catalonia (2019).

- CEO of Falcon Padel S.L. brand.

ACKNOWLEDGEMENTS

Padel is a relatively young sport. The way of playing, the rules and even the structure of the court have evolved radically in recent years.

This book tries to show a way to play this fun sport tactically, applying mechanisms and moves that allow the player to gain more points.

I thank all the coaches who have been part of my learning and have allowed me to develop this way of analysing padel.

Jaume Carreras

Albert Nogueras

Pablo Crosetti

Pablo Aymá

Nico Gavino

Xavi Figols

Photographs taken by Valentí Enrich (@sportvalen)

A guide to improve your level

The real voyage of discovery consists not in seeking new lands but seeing with new eyes.

Marcel Proust

THE SECRETS OF PADEL

INDEX

How this handbook/manual is organised 9

10 general concepts 11

Initiation (I) 19

    What is your goal? 19

    What can help you? 19

    The backhand shot 20

    The placement of the body 21

    How to execute the service? 21

Initiation (II) 23

    Goal: winning the net 23

    The importance of arriving on time 23

    The tilting 24

    How can I get the net back? 24

    What happens if the ball is not easy? 26

    How do we generate an easy ball? 26

    Bandeja shot 27

    Tips on the material 28

Intermediate 29

    Let's improve the service! 29

    The importance of forming a team 30

    Modalities of service: normal and australian 32

    The tactical game. Choosing directions: down the line or cross court? 36

    Theory of angles 37

A guide to improve your level

Effects theory (smashes): the clock 38

Bandeja goals 39

Initiation to the high ball off the back glass (bajada de pared) 43

The mood factor 44

Advanced 46

Tactics applied in the service 46

Roles and functions of each player 48

Generating easy balls in defence and the high backhand volley 49

Types of lobs 52

Ways to win the net 53

Adaptation to external factors 58

Useful accessories 61

Perfection in attacking shots 61

Read the game and analyse the opponents 64

Professional 66

Service and mechanise possible openings 66

Do not abuse the game pattern 69

Play with the scoreboard and have aces up your sleeve 70

Go up late to block or back down 72

Shot preparations that cause the opponents to hesitate 73

Excellence in the smashes and its variants 75

Cutting the opponents' time is necessary 79

Iron mentality. Analyse everything that happens around us 80

THE SECRETS OF PADEL

A guide to improve your level

HOW THIS MANUAL IS ORGANISED

The structure of this manual is easy and simple. It is organised on different levels. Each level has a colour, so it will be easier for you to identify it.

Remember that the improvement process in padel, like in any other sport, is a journey with many ups and downs, but above all, a process of self-improvement. Do not forget that with effort, dedication and desire, you can reach your highest level!

So, now you may be wondering… And how do I start? Well, very easy! You just have to follow these simple steps:

1. KNOW THE GENERAL CONCEPTS OF PADEL

It is essential that you know all the basic concepts of padel. Each and every one of them is necessary to improve. This information will help you understand the whys and *wherefores* of padel, the positioning and the nuances of the shots. It will also allow you to understand the general tactical structure of this sport, many of the decisions that are made on the court and the particularities of each match.

2. CONSOLIDATE THE CONCEPTS OF THE FIRST LEVELS

How? Starting at the beginning. Once you have read it, if you discover that you have learned all the concepts of the first level, it will be much easier for you to understand the following levels.

This manual will allow you to learn and understand the vast majority of concepts that revolve around this sport.

Of course, the level of each player will have a lot to do with the hours of practice of this knowledge on the court.

But the most important thing is to understand that no matter how long a person has been playing padel and playing matches, if these concepts are not known, the improvement process will be much slower and inefficient.

3. GET TO THE END

If you reach the end of this book, it will mean that your level of knowledge about the game is much higher than average. Although the level of play on court is initial, the structure of this book allows you to understand the concepts of the more advanced levels.

With these concepts, you will understand all the commentators of the matches and you will know how to interpret the tactics of your favourite players. And if your talent emerges with the hours of dedication and training, who knows? You may even become a padel star!

Dear reader, you are ready to start!

A guide to improve your level

10 GENERAL CONCEPTS

1 - MEASURES

It is important to understand that **the court** measurements are 20 metres IN A STRAIGHT LINE and 22,36 metres **diagonally**, therefore there is more distance when playing cross court. This information will help us in later chapters to understand court positioning and nuances in different shots.

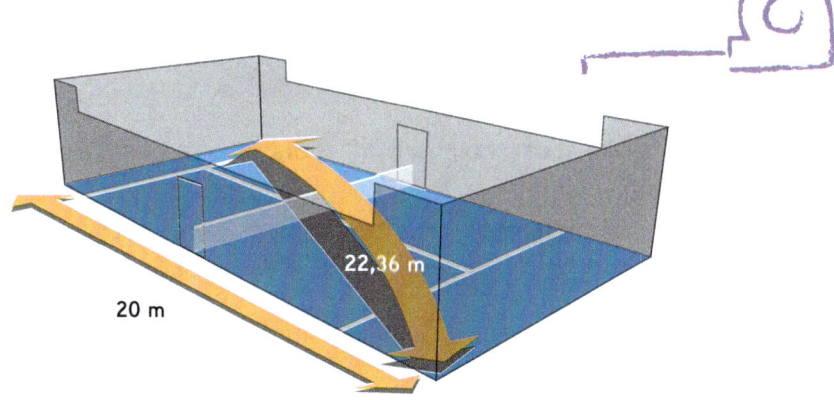

2 - THE NET

The net measures 88 cm **in the centre** and 92 cm at the **ends**. It is therefore better to begin by playing balls over the centre of the net as this increases the probability of more balls being in-play as opposed to playing at the ends where the net is higher. Also, playing across the court, forces you to go through the **centre point of the net** where the net is **4 cm lower**.

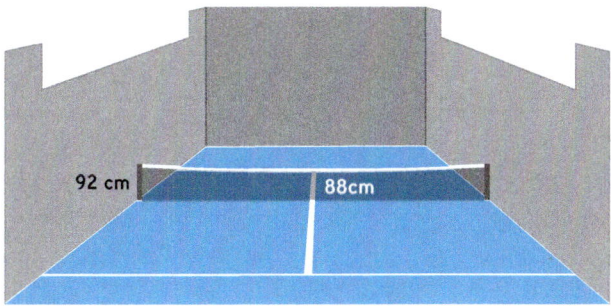

THE SECRETS OF PADEL

3 - TYPES OF SHOTS: BASIC, INTERMEDIATE AND SPECIAL SHOTS

We can classify the shots into three types: **basic, intermediate** and **special** shots.

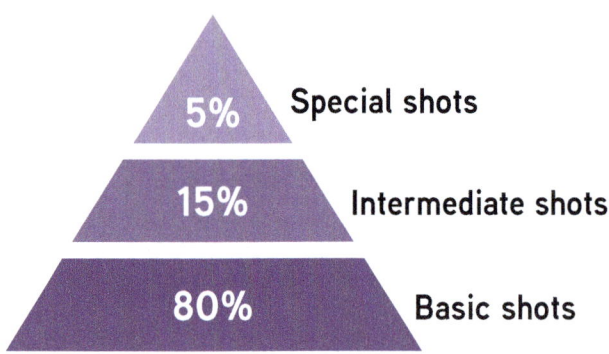

Basic shots are **the most executed of shots** whether practising or playing a match. Having more control over them will always help the final result. Basic shots include the **service, the forehand and backhand drives with or without walls,** the **forehand volley**, backhand volley and the **lob ("Basic Shots")**.

The **Intermediate shots** are used less in comparison to the Basic Shots, As the playing level increases, these intermediate shots start to make more of a difference in the game, and in professional levels they seem to become basic shots for the player. Intermediate shots are the ***Bandeja*** or the **Víbora** and forehand or backhand using the **side wall** or **double wall**.

The **Special shots** are the least used, they can be understood as **defence or attack resources** that are not essential for a beginner. In advanced and professional levels, they could unbalance a match. Examples include the **Smash (and its variations)** or the **Drop Shot** (dejada).

As the playing level improves, more shots are considered basic. With shots such as the *Bandeja* or the Vibora, these are shots which end up being essential at advanced levels.

> **NOTE:** The **high ball off the back glass** (bajada de pared/bajada) can be an intermediate or special shot, depending on the type of player and their ability/game characteristics. The alternative to use *bandeja* with jump or the daring to perform smash variants from afar, with the importance of not losing the net, makes that at a professional level there are players who do not use the bajada often and other players who use it more frequently.

> **NOTE:** The back-wall boast (**contrapared**) has lost relevance with the evolution of the sport. In today's padel it's mostly used as a trick rather than a general stroke. Its execution at the professional level is often a symptom of being late to the ball or being in an uncomfortable situation.

4 - ZONES

There are three main game zones: the **defence zone**, the **attack zone** and the **intermediate zone**.

The **defence** zone comprises the **space between the service line and the back wall**. It is the starting area to return the opponent's service. It is recommended to be between 40 cm and 95 cm **behind the service line**, and closer to the side glass than to the centre of the court. We call the T zone the centre of the court where the serve lines meet. From this zone, the balls that have previously bounced are usually returned. We can help ourselves with the glass for its return according to the depth of the bounce, but always hitting the ball before it bounces a second time.

The **attack zone** is the **space near the net**. It is recommended to be between 3 and 1,5 metres from the net before the opponent hits the ball. The **exact area** will depend on **various factors**. From basic factors such as the **height of each player** or whether the ball is cross or parallel, to factors such as the quality of the ball or the wind.

The **intermediate or transition zone** is the space that exists between the defence zone and the attack zone. At early and intermediate levels, it is recommended not to be there at the moment the opponent executes the shot. It is usually a **transit zone** in the course of winning or losing the net, or to return a ball that forces us to move. It is the area where the smashes (**bandeja**, **smash** or **víbora shot**) are usually executed.

The left side of the court is often called the **ad side**, while the right side of the court is often called the **deuce side** or the equals side.

THE SECRETS OF PADEL

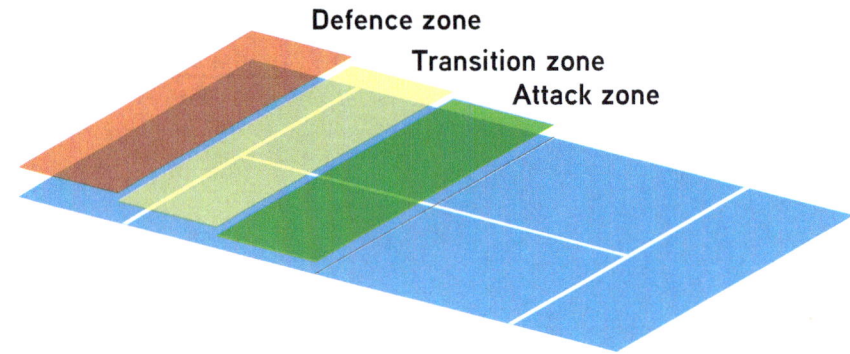

5 - EFFECTS

Ways of hitting shots: **flat shot, topspin effect** and **backspin effect**. In section 3 of this chapter we have presented different movements that exist in this sport.

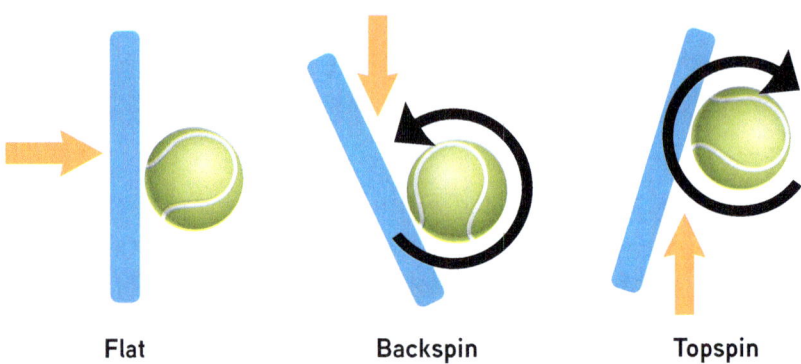

The **flat shot** is the most common and easiest way to hit the ball. It is executed by hitting the central or back part of the ball without generating any forward or backward rotation. Therefore, the **racket/bat preparation** has to be at the **same height as the ball** (on the following pages we are going to say **padel bat** or **padel racket** indistinctly).

It is the type of shot with which people usually have **more precision,** and it can also be executed at a **higher speed**. This shot causes the ball to have a **linear trajectory** and that the ball descends due to the same deceleration and force of gravity. The bounce of the ball on the ground or glass is not modified.

A guide to improve your level

The **topspin shot** is one that occurs when the ball **spins forward**. Its execution is in an upward direction to hit the upper part of the ball. For that reason, the **bat preparation** has to be **below the height of the ball**.

This effect causes the ball to have a **trajectory in the form of** ⌒. In other words, the ball will first take a downward angle, which will allow us to go over the net so that it can quickly go down to the opponents' court.

The ball **bounces more** once it hits the ground or the glass.

The backspin **effect** occurs when the ball **spins backwards**. Its execution is in a downward direction to hit the bottom of the ball. Therefore, the **preparation of the bat** has to be **above the ball**.

The **main characteristic** of this effect is that the ball tends to **slip and bounce less** when it hits the ground or the glass.

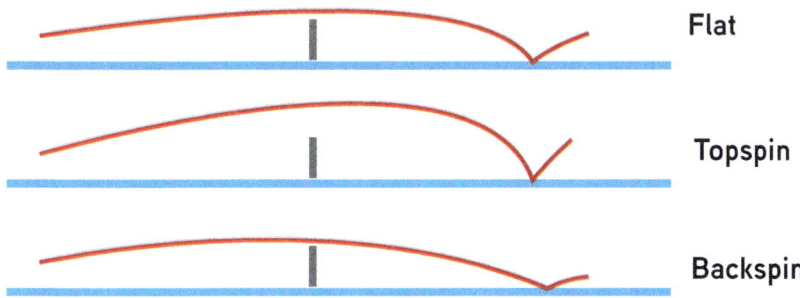

6 - FACTORS THAT AFFECT THE REBOUND

Factors that affect the rebound of the ball. It is important to differentiate between factors that the player can modify when hitting the ball (**internal factors**) and factors that are usually constant and that the player cannot change (**external factors**).

The **internal factors** are: the height of impact of the ball, the depth of the bounce, the power and the effects of the shot.

THE SECRETS OF PADEL

The **external factors** are, among others: the temperature, the quality of the balls, the altitude of the area, the type of grass, the glass, the humidity...

- They favour creating **greater bounce**: higher impact height, greater power, greater depth, topspin effect, higher temperature, new balls, used grass, higher altitude at sea level in the area...

- They cause the ball to **bounce less**: lower impact height, less power, less depth, backspin effect, lower temperature, old balls, new grass, lower altitude at sea level in the area...

> **NOTE:** The impact height will be the most important internal factor, since it will allow us to choose the depth we want to a greater or lesser extent and it will make it easier for us to hit the ball with the effect we want to use.

7 - ATTENTION

Although it seems obvious, padel is a sport where every time a point is started, someone loses it and someone wins it. **Missing means your opponent wins a point**. It cannot be tied. **Be careful with the risk you assume** when you hit, because it could be that your opponent wins points without doing anything at all.

Imagine that in a football match, every time you shoot at goal and don't score, it's a goal for the opponents team...

8 - PARTS OF THE EXECUTION OF A STROKE

In the execution of a shot, we can differentiate three parts that characterise the movement:

a) **Preparation**: it will allow us to have more strength to hit the ball. The more preparation, the greater the ability to push hard.

b) **Point of impact**: impacting the ball further forward or backwards will make us vary the direction in which the ball is going to go.

A guide to improve your level

c) **Termination**: we can improve control by the depth of our stroke. A good completion of the shot will help avoid injuries. If we hit the ball without a proper termination, we will have a sudden impact on our arm, shoulder or body.

Preparation Point of impact Termination

9 - HOW TO ADDRESS THE BALL

To hit the ball and **direct it down the line or cross court**, it is important to understand that it is best to take into account the **point of impact**. We mean hitting the ball earlier or later, or hitting the ball in front of the body or further back. You have to **watch out for** wanting to change the direction of the ball **using sharp turns with the wrist** or the arm. You have to adapt the position of your body according to the point of impact you want to get!

Standing on your side when hitting will allow you to have **more precision** with your shots. Especially when we want to shoot straight, if we stand on our side, it will be important to hit the ball when it is between the two feet, at navel height.

THE SECRETS OF PADEL

> **NOTE:** At advanced and professional levels, faking gestures and directions will be common, but at those levels the precision of the players is very high and they need to surprise or disturb the opponent. In the same way that turning to the side to hit is not always done. Especially when you have to reach difficult balls or anticipate.

10 - FACTORS THAT INFLUENCE THE LEVEL OF A PLAYER

Which factors influence the **total level of a player**? Many people value the technical aspect above all else and this sport really is the sum of many factors. Good agility, resistance, concentration, motivation, strategies and tactics are aspects to take into account.

In this book, we will explain many tactical and strategic concepts that will help you improve the mental aspect. In addition, your technical gestures will be more effective. Even the physical aspect will be affected by understanding positions on the court and understanding more efficient ways to move.

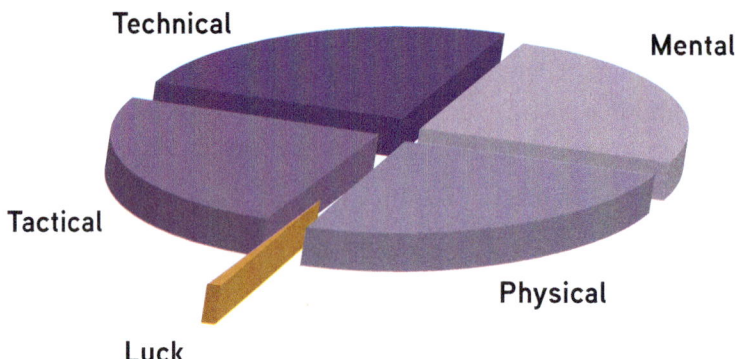

INITIATION (I)

We are at an initial level where we will have to start improving from some very basic premises.

WHAT IS YOUR GOAL?

As our **accuracy is very low**, we will have to focus all our **efforts on not missing**. We will have to limit our intentions, **not to take risks**, passing the ball to the other side of the net will be our main mission. In the next level, Initiation (II), we will begin to explain the importance of winning the net and getting into the attack zone. At the moment, we repeat, try your best to return the ball and gain confidence, even if it is only from the defence zone.

To do so, we will use **flat shots**, explained in section 5 of general concepts. Aiming for the centre of the court will help us reduce the risks and have a higher percentage of hits!

Remember that the net is lower in the middle than on the sides! Also, we won't be afraid of the ball going straight to the side of the court.

The **shots** that we will practice the most are the **basic ones**. The drive and the backhand from the baseline and with glass will have to become more technical, as these movements are the main basis of the defence game.

It is important to understand that **the glasses and the fence** are parts of the court that **can help you** to return balls more easily.

WHAT CAN HELP YOU?

From an optimistic point of view, we have three aids: the back wall, the side wall and the net.

Clearly, returning balls with the **back wall** is much easier, you have to understand that it is a **great help** that will allow you to have **more time** to return balls and increase your accuracy. Therefore, avoiding playing with the back wall is a bad decision. At a more advanced level, we can have the dilemma of letting the ball go against the glass or anticipating (with a volley or a half volley) to cut down the opponent's time.

But, at the current level, **it is better to have more time to think**, playing with the walls will allow us to have an extra time to return fast and deep balls, which will increase our hit rate.

The **side wall** is a **help but to a lesser extent** than the back wall. This does not mean that we should refuse to let the ball go against the side wall but **sometimes it will be preferable to anticipate** and hit with a direct forehand or backhand shot (without the wall).

Also, on days when the ball is wet or humid, the side wall will become very difficult to predict. This is why anticipating and avoiding the side wall is sometimes a good solution.

In any case, **starting to become familiar with the rebound of the side wall** will help us to not be a difficult ball at more advanced levels.

The **randomness of the rebound** that occurs when a ball hits **the fence** will be the main reason why we will **try to avoid the ball hitting there** on most occasions.

Warning! On balls that we would never get to, **the fence can help us**, as the rebound can come up unexpectedly and give us that extra time that will allow us to get there and even move into an advantageous position.

The fence doesn't always work against the defender! It is often **the source of complaints from many players** who appeal to the **bad luck** of the rebound whenever it is not in their favour. You have to understand that the rebound can sometimes help you and sometimes not, accepting this concept will allow you to be **emotionally stable** in a game when other players might get angry and this might affect their level of play.

THE BACKHAND SHOT

If you're having trouble with your **backhand shot**, it is now the best time to practice it. It doesn't matter if you have fewer shots. Keep in mind that in this sport it is not enough to just know how to hit a forehand shot, because as your level improves, your opponents will direct the balls where it bothers you the most and you will not be able to avoid it.

Initiation (I)

If you have little strength with the backhand shot, **you can do it with two hands**. Especially without walls, more and more professional players use this type of shot, although in the medium term, you will have to gain skills and strength with one hand to use in shots apart from the backhand shot.

THE PLACEMENT OF THE BODY

As we explained in the general concepts section, **turning to the side** will allow your **accuracy to increase**. You will have more control over the point of impact of the ball and you will be able to start knowing how to direct your shots to one side of the court or the other. It is important to try to turn on your side as many times as you can! It is common at these levels to **make the mistake of hitting the ball in any way** or the way we should move least! It is a mistake, as you may save a step but your precision will be greatly affected!

Moving **very frequently with constant short steps** will allow you to **improve body posture** when hitting and **correct your position** in the event that the ball goes where you are not expecting.

Although the steps preferably have to be short (except for those balls that are very far away), it is highly recommended that **the last step**, with which you are going to hit, **be wider to have greater stability** in the movement. Impacting the ball with the feet very close together causes little firmness and stability in your movement. Spreading your legs will help you have **more precision**.

Understanding the factors that cause a ball to bounce more or less, explained in the general concepts section, will allow you **to know in advance how the ball is going to bounce** and you will be able to **adjust your position** to hit it at the exact moment and place without having to go late.

HOW TO EXECUTE THE SERVICE?

The **serve**, the responsibility of starting the point having two attempts. We are at a level where many players will try to execute a first serve with a lot of risk trying to win the point directly. By risk we mean increasing power, looking for a lot of placement or giving the ball more spin.

THE SECRETS OF PADEL

We are at a level where it is likely that we will win many direct points by increasing the risk in our service, but we have to be aware that we will win many points for the simple fact that **our opponent,** being also a beginner, **will also fail** many returns.

The fact of **risking a lot on the first service** will mean that there will be **more errors in our serve.** Therefore, we will end up serving more times with second serve. Then, the **fear** of **double faulting** and losing the point will make us serve a **weak second serve**. Many players will end up going from one extreme to the other, from a very aggressive first serve to a harmless second serve.

We recommend you look for a middle ground of risk and try to serve in the most correct way possible. That means avoiding serving with awkward postures, jerky gestures and made-up shots.

Try to **stand on your side**, mechanise a fluid movement in which there is rotation in your shoulders and gain confidence and precision with the movement. It is important that you start trying to **hit the ball at waist height and away from the body**. The regulations do not allow to serve hitting the ball with a higher height. This is why,

you have to understand that if the regulations prohibit this, it is because the higher the service is made, the more aggressive it can be and the greater advantage the server has.

So don't invent weird gestures where the impact is very low and far from waist height and let alone perform half volley services. The service will be legal but you will not improve it.

INITIATION (II)

We are still at an initial level but the hours and our skills have increased.

We have **low accuracy**, but it is no longer a challenge for us to return most of the balls. In any case, we have to continue to focus our **efforts on not failing**. At this level, we will begin to see the importance of winning the net and getting into the attack zone. From the attack zone, we will use volleys (voleas) and smashes.

Without going into nuances of whether we execute cut trays (*bandejas*), vipers (*víboras*) or smashes, our **goal** in the **attack zone** will be to return the ball without previously letting it bounce. You will notice that the points in favour are easily made, since we will be shortening the opponent's reaction time. Remember that from the defence zone we have more time to react, but we have to be aware of the bounce of the ball, the rebound of the wall, make sure that the ball doesn't get complicated after the side wall or the side fence. Instead, from the attack zone, we will simplify our entire game.

GOAL: WINNING THE NET

The **serve** is the first starting point to win the net. We have to start to understand that the serve is not so important when it comes to trying to make the point but it has a **tactical relevance: winning the net**.

THE IMPORTANCE OF ARRIVING ON TIME

First important concept: once we hit the ball, we will have to reach the net zone or attack zone (see exact position in section 4 of general concepts), **BEFORE** the opponent hits the ball.

This concept will be very relevant at all levels. The time that elapses from when we hit the ball until the opponent is about to hit is the time that we have to get into the next position we want to be in.

THE SECRETS OF PADEL

Therefore, if the opponent hits the ball and we are still moving, it is a sign that something is not quite right.

For this reason, we will have to try to serve in such a way that allows us to **reach the attack zone in time** and we can **volley in good conditions**. Although we will not have much control with the volleys and you may even think that staying in the background would earn us more points, insist on practising the volley. You will notice that, when mastering the volleys, earning points will be much easier and simpler.

THE TILTING

The fact of being in the net will mean that many times the balls will pass between you and your partner and you have to run backwards. We will begin to find the importance of **tilting the position and closing the centre area of the court**. The opponents will start to lift the ball and hit lobs. Depending on how good these lobs are, you will have to start making trays (*bandejas*), smashes or letting the ball bounce.

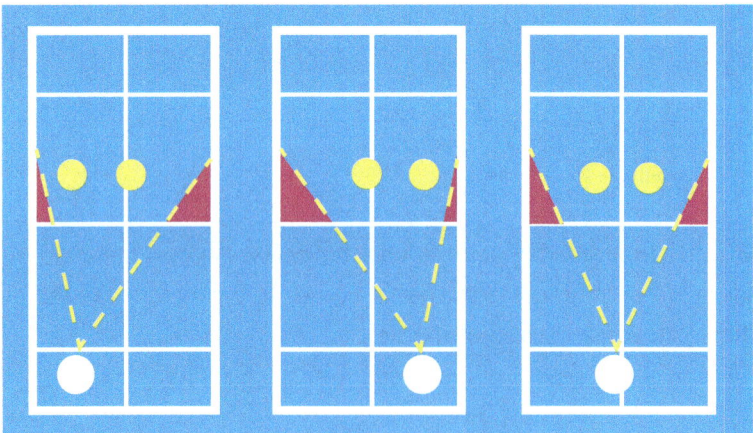

Letting the ball bounce will mean losing the net in the event that the opponent goes up to the attack zone.

HOW CAN I GET THE NET BACK?

So, what do we have to do when we don't have the net? Not having the net implies being in the defence zone. Dominating and gaining confidence with

Initiation (II)

volleys (*voleas*) will imply that **we want to be in the attack zone**, that we want to win the net. Our tactics and ways to achieve it will be the following:

SITUATION 1 - If we are in the defence zone but one of the opponents is not at the net or both are not, we will execute a shot from below (other than a lob) towards the opponent who is not at the net and we will go up. Remember, try to get to the net just before your opponent is going to hit the ball again!

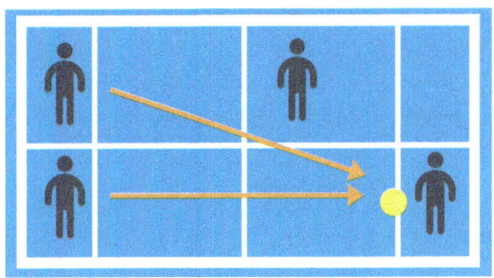

SITUATION 2 - If we are in the defence zone but both opponents are at the net, generally, we will have to hit lobs when the ball is **easy** and wait for it to bounce behind the opponent. We can also wait for one of our shots to pass through the sides or through the middle of the opponents partner (passing shot) and take the opportunity to go up, although it will be less likely.

In situation 2, we have highlighted that **the ball has to be easy to hit a lob**.

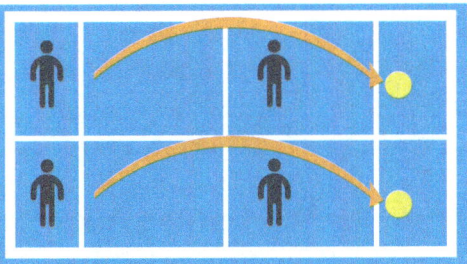 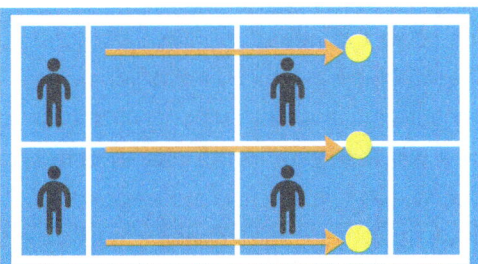

25

THE SECRETS OF PADEL

> **NOTE:** At more advanced levels, we will see more ways to win the network. Going up to the net to block/volley (*volear*) the opponent's tray (*bandeja*), playing low and going to the volleys battle or using *chiquitas* will be common alternatives.

WHAT HAPPENS IF THE BALL IS NOT EASY?

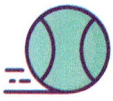

It is one of the fundamental pillars of this sport, and one of the main concepts that intermediate and advanced players forget or have not yet understood.

If the ball that comes to us is not easy and, therefore, we consider it difficult, we will have to play low and try to generate an easy ball.

HOW DO WE GENERATE AN EASY BALL?

When we play low we have two options: let the opponent volley (*volear*) forehand/drive or backhand. Generally, our opponents will deal more damage to us with a forehand volley than a backhand volley. Therefore, it is very important to observe if the opponents are right-handed or left-handed to **locate their backhand volleys** and try to intentionally direct the balls there.

On the other hand, another way to get easy balls is to **execute faster low shots**, so the opponents will have less time to react and will probably end up playing a worse volley. The problem with speeding up is taking more risk and making more errors.

It will also be more difficult for the opponent to volley the ball **the closer it comes to the net** or the lower it goes. That will increase their fear of throwing the ball into the net, which will mean they will volley up with less velocity. Clearly, we will also be increasing the risk, in this case, of throwing it directly into the net.

> **NOTE:** In later chapters we will discuss playing low to the opponent's high backhand volley. We will see that it is a very effective variant to generate easy balls at advanced or professional levels. Levels where it will be increasingly difficult to find easy balls.

Initiation (II)

In the same way that in the previous chapter (Initiation (I)) we told you to begin to gain confidence with volleys, in this chapter, you will have to do the same with the *bandeja* shot.

BANDEJA SHOT

The **bandeja** is a shot that it's made in the attack zone or intermediate zone. It is a shot that is executed once the opponent (who is in the defence zone) shoots us a lob to win the net. If the opponent's lob is not perfect, we can move backwards to try to return the ball without it bouncing. We will have to try to start hitting the ball above eye level so as not to have as much risk of throwing it into the net. When you set up the shot, bring your elbow up to shoulder height and try to get on your side to execute this punch (righties, left leg in front, and lefties, right leg in front).

Once the *bandeja* shot has been executed, the goal is to go back up to the attack zone and continue winning the net. This shot will be very important at later levels and we will clarify ways and intentions of executing it. For now, try to practice this shot to gain coordination.

In the event that the opponent's lob is very good and we cannot make the *bandeja* shot, basically, it will mean that we are already in the back zone or defence zone. So we will let it bounce and we will execute another lob or return it from below (**bajada de pared**) before or after the ball hits the wall.

> **NOTE:** The **bajada de pared** (high ball off the back glass) is an offensive shot that is made from the defence zone. As it is a more complicated execution shot since it has a higher risk, we will introduce its explanation in later levels. As an alternative to the **bajada**, you can usually always throw another lob at the opponent to try to win the net again, in case the opponents have gone up to the net.

TIPS ON THE MATERIAL

At these levels, if we start playing for many hours, it is important that we start giving more importance to the material we play with. Bear in mind that we are at a low technical level, that means that many shots are not correct, which causes the body, and especially the arm area, to suffer a lot.

To avoid pain and injuries, it is advisable to play with lightweight rackets/bats (340-360 grams) which are not extremely hard. Since you are getting into this sport, it is better to prevent injuries. Therefore, it is recommended not to use a very hard racket.

Regarding sports shoes, the more engraved and relief the sole has, the better. It is best to play with herringbone sole shoes.

INTERMEDIATE

After hours and hours of practice, we are already at the **intermediate level**! This level is characterised by the fact that both our rivals and us do not fail excessively. The points start to last and have a little tactical structure. You will notice that physically we are starting to get more tired!

We have an **average precision**, each time we dare to make strokes with a little more risk. The fundamental thing to advance in level will be that we are consistent with the risk of our shots and begin to have greater tactical discipline. We will have to understand that it is one thing to miss the shot and another to miss the choice. Choosing and having an adequate shot intention will greatly increase the percentage of success and we will win games without complicating ourselves.

LET'S IMPROVE THE SERVICE!

Let's start with the **service**. In the previous level, we have acquired the mechanics of serving and getting to the net. Now that we have more accuracy with our forehand and backhand volleys (*voleas*), we need to focus on our next improvements.

It is just as important to execute a good serve as it is to execute a good first volley. For that, we will have to try to mechanise a service with which while we hit the ball we already start the race towards the net. Thus, we can get to the attack zone sooner. Important: the **goal** is to get to the attack zone just before my opponent returns the ball.

We will have to improve our **serve using the backspin effect** so that the ball stays low and my opponent receives a difficult ball. Remember that, if the rival gets a difficult ball, he will not be able to make a good lob and that way we will not lose the net so easily.

Do not think that the **service** only hurts by taking out the side wall. Taking out the **opponent's body** or the **T zone** are equally effective variants. For example, taking out the T zone and then volleying to the corner is a very good option, since by taking out the T zone we will move our rival to the centre of the court and the corner will be uncovered.

We have to start mastering the service with the Australian modality, especially if a left-hander and a right-hander play together.

THE SECRETS OF PADEL

THE IMPORTANCE OF FORMING A TEAM

Have you considered the importance of both being right-handed, left-handed or one left-handed and one right-handed in a team?

Normally, your most effective volleys are forehand volleys and your least favourite volleys are backhand volleys, right?

Let's imagine that you **are two right-handers** and you are in the attack zone. We observe that the player in the backhand zone (left zone of the court) covers the centre with his forehand volley or forehand. But we see that his partner, the player on the right, covers his central zone with his backhand volley.

If our rivals are in the defence zone, remember that they will generally shoot us at our backhand volley, because it is supposed to be our least effective shot and thus they will generate easy balls. Then, our rivals, playing in the centre of the court, will find a backhand volley, the one of the player on the right.

But if they want to hit the backhand volley of the player on the left it will be a bit more risky, because it is located near the side of the court, which will less encourage the opponent to direct balls there for fear of missing the shot.

However, the player parallel to our left player will have an easier time directing balls at our backhand volley since he will only have to shoot in a straight line.

Intermediate

Now let's imagine that you **are two lefties** and you are in the attack zone. We observe that the player in the backhand zone (left zone of the court) covers the centre with his backhand volley. But we see that his partner, the player on the right, encompasses his central area with his forehand volley.

In the same way as in the case of the two right-handers, **the central area will be covered by a drive volley and a backhand volley**. Thus, our defending rivals will more easily direct their returns towards the backhand volley of our player on the left, because this backhand volley occupies the central zone and it is not risky to shoot towards it.

Our player on the right will have his backhand volley close to the lateral zone, therefore the rivals will have to be more vigilant if they want to direct balls towards us, since there is a greater risk of making mistakes because the ball may deflect to the lateral zone directly.

It should be noted that the rival parallel to our forehand player will find it easier to direct balls at our backhand volley since he will only have to shoot in a straight line.

But what would happen with a **pair of right-handed and left-handed**? If the right-hander plays in the left area of the court and the left-hander in the right area, we observe that the centre area of the court is covered by the drive of each player, the shots that tend to be more effective. Therefore, if the defenders want to direct the balls into their backhand volleys, they will have to take more risk as they will have to direct them closer to the lateral zone.

What if these players, right-handed and left-handed, play in the other zone? That is, the left-hander in the left area of the court and the right-hander in the right area. Well, when they are in the attack zone, the entire central zone of the court will be occupied by their weakest shots! Then the rival pair, shooting to the centre and without risking, will be able to find their backhand volleys, which will allow them to generate more easy balls and, thus, be able to shoot better lobs and win the net earlier.

In this way, we begin to see that playing in one area or another of the court has a very important relevance. Padel rules require us to stay on the same side throughout the set. Therefore, we must decide in our first game which zone we want to occupy since it will condition us for many games.

On the other hand, when we are serving, depending on the type of service we want to use, we can play the point in one area of the court or another.

MODALITIES OF SERVICE: NORMAL AND AUSTRALIAN

Let us imagine that the pair to be analysed are right-handed and left-handed. The right-handed player is about to start the game with his serve. Being 0-0, the service has to be from the right side of the court and go towards the rival left box.

Intermediate

With the **normal modality**, our left-handed partner would be placed at the net in the left area of the court. The right-handed player would serve and go up to the net staying in the right box.

Thus, the centre would be covered only by backhand volleys, bad business.

Using the **Australian modality** would mean that at 0-0, this right-handed player who is about to serve would be placed in the right zone of the court but right next to the T zone. His left-handed partner would be placed in the right box. When serving, the server would go up to the left side of the court, which would allow the centre of the court to be covered by two drive volleys. Problem solved.

We will be able to use the Australian modality whenever we want, not only because we are left-handed and right-handed, but also because you are beginning to specialise in a certain area of the court or because, as a couple, it is better for you to be on one side than the other due to your characteristics of play.

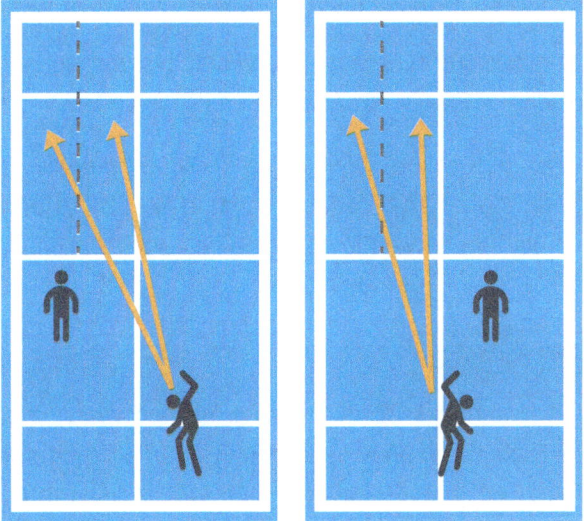

Padel rules force us to serve in a cross direction and we would be respecting it. We would only be placing ourselves in the T zone to get to the area we want sooner!

THE SECRETS OF PADEL

It seems that it is clear that, if a left-hander and a right-hander play together, the optimal thing would be for the left-hander to play on the right side and the right-hander on the left side, in order to have the centre of the court covered by two forehand volleys.

But what happens if we are two righties or two lefties? Who plays on the left or on the right?

Various factors will cause us to end up deciding which of the two players is preferable to play in a specific area.

IN THE CASE OF A COUPLE OF TWO RIGHT-HANDERS

1-With very different levels.

To do this, you have to start by understanding that the player who is going to play on the left of the court is going to have his forehand stroke in the centre of the court. His more skillful arm will be closer to the dividing centre line.

Therefore, it will be easier for him to go in and help his partner on the right. With a few steps and stretching out his arm, he will enter his court.

So, in general, we can deduce that if two players have different levels, the better one would have to play on the left to be able to come in to help his partner. It would be rare that the player with the lowest level had to be aware of helping the good one.

2-With slightly different levels.

If the level of a player is not far from the level of his partner, it is likely that there are cases in which both are already used to playing in a specific area of the court. In other words, it may be that the lower level player is used to playing on the left and the higher level player is used to playing on the right and they add more as a couple playing in their usual areas.

In any case, if this pair were to play against two rivals who had the same level, they would have to develop tactics so that the player with the higher level touched more balls.

3-With identical levels.

If a pair of right-handers has an apparently identical level and perform in a similar way on both sides of the court, we will have to qualify the following factors:

→It is recommended that the player with the best attack plays in the left zone of the court. Since, at the net zone, the greatest volume of balls usually pass through the centre and this player (the one who plays in the left zone) could touch a greater number of balls, in addition to being able to enter the court of his partner to help him with his forehand or with his shot in case his rivals execute a lob.

→What if two players attack the same way? We choose to play on the left the person who is physically in better condition. Being two right-handers, the player on the left has to help the player on the right in those balls that remain uncomfortable in his backhand volley zone. Usually, if the level of the two is the same, the taller player will have an easier time attacking better, since he will miss the net less when the other pair shot lobs at him. Therefore, he will be able to cover his area and the T zone, causing his rivals not to find as many directions to throw the lob.

NOTE: In the case of two left-handed players, the criteria to be taken into account will be the same as in the case of two right-handed players but putting the left-hander who is of a higher level or the one who attacks better on the right side of the court so that he can help covering the centre area.

THE TACTICAL GAME. CHOOSING DIRECTIONS: DOWN THE LINE OR CROSS COURT?

Being four players on the court and having two rivals in front of us, we can choose to play down the line or cross court. In this next section, we will assess the advantages and disadvantages of taking one of these two options.

The most obvious tactic, and a great reason for choosing to shoot cross court or down the line may be that one of the two rivals is superior to the other. So, if we want to win, it is normal for us to think about **throwing the ball to the lower level player**, since there is a greater chance that he misses.

But what if the two rivals have a similar level?

The easiest thing in this sport is to attack cross court and defend down the line.

When we are at the net, in the volley zone, **if we hit cross court we will have more metres and more angle**! In the section of general concepts, we clarify that in crossed, for a geometric question, **there is more space**. This can allow us to have more margin and shoot harder.

But, above all, in cross court we have more angle. It means it will be **less risky to aim for the side of the court** without missing as much, and thus more likely to win the point.

So, if the player prefers to attack cross court for the reasons above, the defender has to prioritise playing down the line to create space.

All padel players have **more precision aiming at the same area where the ball comes from**. Changing the direction of the ball means aiming where our eyes are not looking. That lowers our accuracy. Can you imagine playing darts and wanting to hit the centre of the target without looking at it? Difficult, isn't it? This does not mean that we always have to shoot to the same area where the ball comes from, but it is a factor to take into account.

Therefore, if the defender throws the ball cross court and the attacker likes to play cross court, the last one will have an easier time. You will only have to repeat the direction from which the ball comes, besides, he will have more metres and angle!

Also, do you remember the tilt discussed in Initiation (II)?

If we are at the net and the ball is held by the rival drive player (the one on the right), our left player will have to approach the left lateral area, leaving a good part of the centre covered by our right player.

But if we are at the net and the ball is held by the rival left player (the one on the left), it will be our drive player who will have to approach the right side area, leaving the centre area covered by our left player.

In this way, if the defenders shot down the line all the time and the attackers all the time cross court, the attackers would always have to be tilting. Moving from one side to the other of the court to close the parallel and central zones (the shooting zones of less risk for our defending rivals).

THEORY OF ANGLES

Attacking cross court will allow us to throw more balls to the lateral areas (side wall or fence) since we will have more metres and **more angle**.

But being near the dividing line is not the same as being near the fence. The closer we are to our side, the more angle we will have to execute our shot towards the rival's opposite side area.

For example, if we are a right-handed player who is attacking from the left side of the court, we will have more angle to play towards the opponent's fence with our backhand cross court volley. As we have our forehand volley in a more centered area, the angle will be smaller and the risk of failure will be higher.

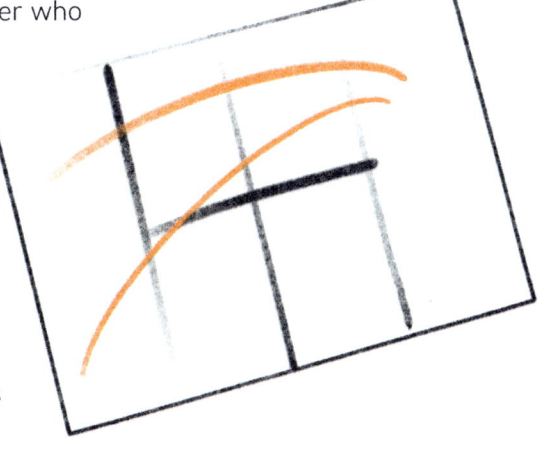

Another different aspect is that we have more skill with one shot than another, but as the hours go by, we will have to try to have the same skill with both the backhand and the forehand because, if not, the rivals will try to throw all their shots to our least skillful zone.

This theory of angles can also be applied when a lob is thrown at us. If we want to shoot towards the rival fence, we will have a higher percentage of success if the lob is received near our lateral zone than if it is thrown at the T zone. These shots to the fence are usually called hooks, rollers or topspins to the fence. Its execution can be flat or topspin, even some professional players shoot with some lateral effects.

Therefore, if we want to execute *bandejas* or shots from the T zone, it is best to aim for the back wall to avoid unnecessary risks.

This intermediate level is characterised by beginning to use the *bandeja* on a regular basis. We players are beginning to have a medium level of control and an increasingly organised tactical structure. The lob is very common, because the attackers usually leave many easy balls to the defenders, therefore the pair that keeps the net longer and has fewer errors ends up dominating the game.

EFFECTS THEORY (SMASHES): THE CLOCK

To easily explain the effects that can be given to the smashes when a ball has been thrown at us, we will have to imagine that the ball is a wall clock.

Therefore, 12 o'clock will be at the top centre, 3 o'clock to the right, 6 o'clock to the bottom centre, and 9 o'clock to the left.

So, we relate the point where we have to hit the ball with the clock time.

Right-handed players have to execute shots hitting the right side of the ball, therefore from 12 o'clock to 6 o'clock. On the other hand, left-handers must hit from the left area of the ball, from 6 o'clock to 12 o'clock.

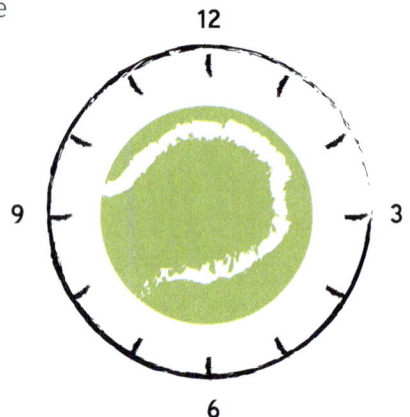

In the case of **right-handers**, if they hit the ball in the area between 12 o'clock and a quarter to 3, we can say that the ball has a forward spin (topspin effect). If they hit the ball in the 3 o'clock area, we can say that the ball has a sidespin (*vibora*). And, if they hit the ball in the area between a quarter past 3 and 6 o'clock, we can say that the ball has a backspin.

At the **advanced level**, we will see nuances of hitting the ball at 12 o'clock, at 1 o'clock and at 2 o'clock, in the same way as in backspin shots, the differences between hitting the ball at 6 o'clock, at 5 o'clock and at 4 o'clock. Each hit will have its characteristics, advantages and disadvantages. We will even see a variant of the smash at a **professional level**, with a right-hander being able to hit in the 11 o'clock zone to take it off the court through the left zone.

In the case of **left-handers**, if they hit the ball in the area between a quarter past 9 and 12 o'clock, we can say that the ball has a forward spin (topspin effect). If they hit in the 9 o'clock area, we can say that the ball has a sidespin (*vibora*). And, if they hit the ball in the area between 6 o'clock and a quarter to 9, we can say that the ball has a backspin.

BANDEJA GOALS

What goals do we have with the *bandeja*? Is it an offensive or defensive shot?

The ***bandeja*** fulfils an essential tactical function in a match: **not to lose the net**. As our level increases, it can be a more and more offensive shot.

For now, at this intermediate level, we should try to use the *bandeja* as a **mechanism to avoid losing the net**. That is to say, after our rival's lob, if we see that by pulling back we can execute a *bandeja*, we will do it and go up to the attack zone again. Generally, we will use *bandeja* (with backspin or flat effect) or *vibora* shot (with sidespin).

We can rank our goals from highest to lowest priority in the following order:

1-Take as few risks as possible so as **not to miss the shot**.

2-After executing the *bandeja*, **go back up to the attack zone**. Recover the net.

3-**That our rival does not have an easy ball left** to overwhelm us with the next shot.

4-With our *bandeja*, being able to **cause the necessary doubts to our rival**, and thus make him consider that the ball that comes to him is difficult, and therefore, **that he cannot comfortably throw a lob at us again**.

THE SECRETS OF PADEL

> **Remember that these goals are ordered from highest to lowest priority,** therefore, if we want to shoot a very risky *bandeja* to complicate the opponent's ball but we forget to go back up to the net, we will be doing it wrong.
>
> Note that we have not set the final goal of winning the point, since at this level it has a clearly tactical function, it is even similar to the tactical function of the service.

TIP to know what risk to assume with our tray

TRAFFIC LIGHT TIP

We are going to present a didactic example of how to know if we can take more or less risk with a *bandeja*. This example can be extended to many padel shots.

Just like a traffic light has the colours **green**, **orange** and **red**, we will try to attribute a colour to each lob that is thrown at us, depending on the difficulty we have in shooting a *bandeja* after that lob.

That is, if the opponent's lob is bad and falls short, it is most likely that we will consider it an easy ball and we will classify it as **green**.

But on the contrary, if the opponent's lob is very good, deep, there is wind or we have the sun in our face, it will be a very difficult ball and we will consider it **red**.

Note that we will not only classify the balls red or green according to their depth, but the most important thing will be that we value them for how we live them at that moment. That is to say, if we are tired, if it is windy, if we do not see the ball well, if we have sweat in our eyes or if we have arrived late to the striking zone, this will also be factors that will make that ball qualify as **red**, regardless of whether it is not an apparently difficult lob.

So, to know what risks to take:

→With **green balls**, we can try to fulfil all the goals of the *bandeja* explained above. Leaving the difficult ball to the opponent can be an easy goal to achieve.

→With **red balls**, we will have to do everything possible to take very few risks so as not to miss the ball. If we win the net again and do not leave an easy ball to the opponent, we can already be satisfied!

→The **orange balls** will be those that are doubtful, that do not seem very difficult but not easy either. The risk to be assumed will have to be consistent. Taking more risks when hitting (shooting harder, with more spin, placing the ball more or dropping the point of impact) an orange ball than a green one would not be very logical.

Surely, many players, depending on whether their mood is good or the score is in their favour, will choose to see them **greener**. Instead, players with low confidence, adverse scores or pressure will see them **redder**.

Another possible option, if we have problems with the **red balls**, is to turn them green. If, for example, we see the opponent's lob as very complicated and deep, we can omit shooting a *bandeja* and let the ball bounce. At that moment, it is most likely that the ball will become easy for us... But be careful, it is most likely that our rival will take advantage of the fact that we have let it bounce and go up to the net. Therefore, **the price we will be paying to go from a red ball to a green one will be to lose the net**. A somewhat expensive price!

In any case, depending on the situation, using the ***bajada de pared*** will be a good solution for these cases in which we have let the opponent's lob bounce. We will explain this shot at the end of this chapter and in the following levels.

TIP to know what risk to take with our shots

MATHS TIP: ADD 10

This didactic example deals with how to know with what risk or intentions we can execute a shot.

It consists of rating the balls between 0 and 10 according to its difficulty. Being 0 a very easy ball to return and 10 a very difficult ball.

In the same way that the intentions or the risk that we can assume with the next ball will have to be measured from 0 to 10. Being 0 a ball with little risk and with very few intentions of winning the point or doing damage on our part and being 10 a very aggressive and risky ball.

So what we have to think about is that the sum of the two grades has to be 10.

Therefore, if we receive a ball rated as 3 (an easy ball to return), we can try to make a shot with intentions and risk of 7.

We would be choosing wrong, if a ball rated as 8 (difficult ball) came to us and we wanted to throw a ball of 9 (an offensive ball on our part). What would happen, surely, is that we would end up failing. It cannot be that we receive a highly complicated ball and want to return a worse one to the rival.

This paradigm is very useful when the level of the 4 players on court is similar. So the rivals sometimes throw balls of 4, 8 or 2. We will have to wait for the right moment and the exact ball to want to take the initiative.

If the rivals are much superior to us, we will find balls from 5 to 10 almost all the time. So, we advise you to continue complying with this tip to try to **make the match last as long as possible. The normal thing is that we lose this match**, but we will have more options and we will learn more if we comply with this tip and put more balls inside.

On the contrary, if we start to execute risky balls bearing in mind that what comes to us is complicated for us, we will end up failing a lot and losing in twenty minutes.

Intermediate

INITIATION TO THE HIGH BALL OFF THE BACK GLASS (*BAJADA DE PARED*)

If we are in the attack zone and the lob that the rival throws at us is so good and deep that we cannot get there to execute a *bandeja*, we may have to let the ball bounce to execute another lob or make a **high ball off the back glass (*bajada de pared*)** after the ball has touched the wall.

The moment we let the opponent's lob bounce, it is most likely that they will go up to the attack zone and we will lose the net. Therefore, shooting another lob to win the net again is always a good option.

But... What if the ball, after bouncing and touching the wall, stays very high, in front of the body and we are well positioned? So, if these three situations occur, we can execute an attack hit called *bajada de pared*. The goal of this shot is to **surprise the opponent**, either with a **power shot** or a **setting shot** to **try to win the point**. In cases where one of the rivals has not risen, hitting the *bajada* with a lot of backspin effect in the direction of that rival will also be a very good option, since we can go back up to the net with the rival in the defence zone with a low and difficult ball.

In the next levels we will expand the ways to execute it and the different situations in which we can find ourselves.

But remember, the *bajada* is one of the few attack hits that is made from the defence zone! It is the last attempt to win the point before we lose the net for good.

In any case, we have to be aware of the risk of shooting it, since we are located very far from the net. Therefore, try to do it only when:

1-We have arrived on time and we are well positioned.

2-The ball remains high (at least more than 120 cm high approximately, remember that the net measures 88 cm in its centre area).

3-The ball stays in front of our body. The ball has to stay between the net and us. If it stays between us and the wall, the difficulty will be very high.

> **These three conditions must all be met!**
>
> If one of them does not occur, it is better that you return to throw another lob and do not use the *bajada*.

THE MOOD FACTOR

Note that, in the tip of the traffic light, we have commented that there is an **emotional factor** that influences the way of assessing the difficulty of the balls or that gives us confidence to make more risky shots. It is important that, at this level, we learn to assess the state of confidence in ourselves, our partner and our rivals.

If we find ourselves 4-0 down and 30/0 down, chances are we won't play loose and feel pressure from the scoreboard. Therefore, we have to learn to reverse these situations, consolidate moments in which we have initiative and good feelings or know how to encourage and get the best out of our partner.

Understanding what state of mind the rival is in will help us to be able to develop more appropriate strategies. We will be able to assess which balls and shots are the ones that are hurting us and which are the result of a state of excessive euphoria.

For example, if the rival is winning and has a score of 40/0 up and shoots a very aggressive volley that he had not done until that moment, it does not have to surprise us and affect us. We cannot draw conclusions from that opponent's shot and come to think that he is suddenly going to volley like this for the rest of the match if he wasn't doing it before.

Intermediate

We would have to worry about the opponent frequently scoring points with his volley with a tight games score of 30/30 or 40/30. Tight scores are the best times to analyse your rivals. It's those situations where points become more important, since the fear of failing and losing the game or having a break ball will make players think more carefully about their decisions.

ADVANCED

Many hours later, after numerous close matches, after attempts to test shots and moves, with numerous strategies used and with many comeback matches thanks to the emotional and mental factor, we are already at the advanced level! This level is characterised by starting to try to make direct points and having a high level of control. With the technique we have, the normal thing is not to miss!

Points can last long, even when hitting aggressive shots. The details make the difference and, above all, **the mental aspect begins to be decisive**. Physically, we are more adapted to this sport, we catch our breath quickly and we can endure long sets without failures appearing due to fatigue problems.

We have a high precision, therefore we assume that we will not miss the ball, we will even try to harm the opponent. To be better at this advanced level, we will have to continue being efficient with the risk of our shots, tactical discipline will be necessary and essential, assessing the moment of the game we are in will help us make the most appropriate decisions which will allow us to start automate plays and moves to gain the point faster.

As in the previous levels, we will start with the **service**. In the previous level, we learned the importance of executing a good serve and a good first volley (*volea*).

TACTICS APPLIED IN THE SERVICE

At this level, we will have to **analyse the rival** before serving and keep a mental statistic of how the previous points went. Although the rival does not have very marked weaknesses, surely we will know how to assess what shots he likes and in what areas he is hurting us.

For example, if we are a left player who is serving and our rivals are right-handed, if we serve with 0/0 (we will be serving from the right zone to the left zone) we can see that if we direct the serve to the side glass, the rival will hit a

Advanced

drive shot, a shot that is usually liked by right-handed players who play on the right side of the court.

Then, we should think things such as:

→If my first serve is very good, as much as he likes to return balls using forehand shots, he will put the racket however he can and we will be able to take the initiative with our first volley.

→Although my serve is good, this rival has a very good forehand shot, every time he is making a good return and I cannot take the initiative.

→Serving to the side wall jeopardises my serve in the Australian modality, as if the receiver steps up and anticipates my serve, it is likely that I will be late at the net or he will hit a **passing shot**.

→This player is playing on the right side of the court but he normally plays on the left side, therefore he is not so specialised in defending in that zone. I will serve to the side wall because he will probably not coordinate the return well.

→The last few serves that I've made, the opponent has returned the ball down the line to my backhand volley. So if he does the same thing now, I'll try to get there earlier and volley backhand to the opposite zone fence.

→This player is returning the ball down the line to my high backhand volley, he disarms me every time and then throws a lob. You know what? I'd better serve to the T zone or to the body.

You should begin to consider all these ideas, as they are very useful and will allow you to begin to draw a **game scheme or pattern** and, above all, to analyse it in order to find solutions when you have adverse moments in the match.

Going with the score in your favour, playing without thinking and still winning is very nice, but when a game gets complicated and the pressure begins to arise, analysing what is happening will give you hope and solutions to fight against these complicated situations.

But we will always have to try to make our best shot. That does not mean that it is the most powerful hit or with the most spin. The best shot will be the one that goes in the right direction, with the right depth, at the right speed and with enough spin.

THE SECRETS OF PADEL

Regarding the service, we will have to try to serve as many times as possible with the first serve due to the psychological effect that we inflict on our opponent. Having a 70% effectiveness with the first serve seems like a very high success rate.

But we will have to assess whether the fact of risking something less will allow us to reach 80% effectiveness or more, in order to be able to serve fewer times with the second serve and keep the rival with the uncertainty of not knowing what quality of the first serve they are going to receive.

Remember that, when the opponent is waiting for the service to return, he usually has a more defensive intention if he waits for a first serve. Instead, when the first serve has been missed, he is often thinking about how to fight back and win the net.

Therefore we can summarise that **the first service is important since it causes mistakes and doubts in the rival for the simple fact of being the first**, although later it is not a great first service.

ROLES AND FUNCTIONS OF EACH PLAYER

Although we have a high level of precision we will have to be aware of our roles in the court. For this, we must clarify what roles are necessary to play in one area or the other of the court.

If we are a right-handed couple

PLAYER ON THE LEFT SIDE. If we play on the left side of the court, it's because we have mainly decided that we attack better. Therefore, the role of earning points and the initiative to push more with the shot or make it difficult for the rival will have to be carried out by us. Although that does not mean that we can risk without sense and allow ourselves to miss.

PLAYER ON THE RIGHT SIDE. If our partner attacks better than us, we will have to adopt a more tactical role in attack. We will prioritise not missing and generating easy balls for my partner. Being both right-handed, my centre zone will be covered by my backhand volley. Therefore, if the rivals have the same level, we will try to play balls towards my opponent in front, so that we tilt to the right and the middle is covered by the forehand shots of my partner (the better attacker of the two).

If we are a left-handed couple

The roles will be the same as the previous ones but the zone will be changed. Remember! The best attacker should play on the right side of the court to cover the centre with his forehand shots.

If one is left-handed and the other is right-handed

We assume that, from the intermediate level, the left-handed player has to go on the right side of the court and the right-handed player has to go on the left side.

Therefore, the most offensive role will have to be played by the player who has the most skill in scoring points. In the event that both attack equally, we will simply have to assess, in the balls that go to the centre, which player is in more advantageous conditions to take on that responsibility.

Just like in a basketball team, to be efficient, the three-point specialist is usually responsible for shooting three-pointers. A good padel partner will have to know which are the best shots of both players and take more responsibilities in those aspects in which each of them is most proficient.

GENERATING EASY BALLS IN DEFENCE AND THE HIGH BACKHAND VOLLEY

In the initiation (II) level, we saw the importance of throwing lobs in padel when, from the defence zone, we have an easy ball and the rivals are at the net.

In this level, we should have variants to the lobs, ways to win the net without throwing lobs and make moves to disturb the rival going to the volleys battle (*choque de voleas*).

Let's remember that it will be more likely to generate easy balls in defence if we execute shots that:

→Go to our opponent's backhand volley.

→Go as forcefully as possible towards the opponent.

→Go as low as possible on the net.

Also remember that in a note we discussed the option of playing towards our opponent's backhand volley but intentionally raising the ball without actually shooting a lob.

Let's also remember that the impact height of the ball is the factor that most influences the rebound. It also conditions the depth with which you will be able to play and makes it impossible to execute some effects.

In volleys, the impact height of the ball will normally be determined and we will be able to vary it a little, since the ball reaches us at a certain speed that prevents us from letting it fall more or catch it earlier. On the other hand, in smashes, when the rival throws lobs at us, we can choose the height of impact we want since, between the time the ball goes up and down, we have time to adapt our position and decide the height of impact.

Therefore, if we are in defence and the rivals are in the attack zone, if we play a high ball to our rival's backhand volley zone, he will not be able to bury the volley with backspin effect, since, no matter how much effect he gives the ball, it will fall

Advanced

too vertical and then go up anyway. Nor will he be able to make an excessive power shot, since normally the backhand shot cannot be done at high speed.

However, we have to keep in mind that the rival will be able to choose how deep to play the next ball and may even have more angle to play towards the lateral zones. We also have to watch at what speed we execute this shot, because if we are raising the ball and we shoot hard, the ball can go directly to the wall. And if we play it very slowly, the rival will be able to invert or move to execute a high forehand volley and he will have a free ball to throw a very aggressive and powerful shot.

Playing the high backhand volley is a very good variant to generate easy balls but you have to be careful how you use it so that you don't lose the point quickly. In addition, it is incompatible with the moves that we will show you below.

For example, throwing a high backhand volley and going up to the volleys battle is not a great choice since the opponent will have an easy time throwing the ball at our feet. Instead, it can be a good way to generate the following move: I throw the ball to my opponent's high backhand volley so I can generate an easy ball and then try to shoot a *chiquita* or a powerful shot to go up to the volleys battle.

If the opponent's high backhand volley is played to generate an easy ball, we have to understand that the previous ball was not easy. It would be illogical to have an easy ball and make a shot to make it easy again. So, do we play high backhand volley when the previous ball is difficult?

Yes, but no. At this level, we don't have to simply classify the balls as easy or difficult. Let's try to rate the balls from 0 to 10. Where 10 is an extremely difficult ball and 0 is a very easy ball. Therefore, at earlier levels, we could say that from 0 to 5 were easy, and from 5 to 10 were difficult. But do you notice that a level 6 ball is not the same as a level 9 ball?

So, as the high backhand is a shot in which you need to have a certain precision, since it may be that we miss it or the opponent hits us a hard forehand. If the ball is deflected, we will try to shoot the high backhand volley when we rate the ball from 5 to 7 to try to generate a ball of lower difficulty. And so, subsequently try to win the net.

TYPES OF LOBS

In padel there are two kinds of lobs: the high lob and the fast lob.

The **high lob** is a lob that is characterised by taking a lot of height. They are usually lobs with heights greater than 7 metres (remember that the court measures 4 metres at its highest bottom area). These lobs are more difficult to control but they cause a lot of difficulties for our rivals since they lose coordination (timing). These lobs will take time to rise and fall, therefore our rivals will have time to go back and be able to choose which shot to execute. But we will also have time to change our position and generate surprise moves such as blocking the *bandeja*.

The **fast lob** is characterised by not taking too much height (between 3 and 4 metres) and being played at a speed that causes our rivals to not have time to put together a good shot, hit badly or even the ball passes them quickly. This lob doesn't catch a lot of parabola and it doesn't take long to start going down, so you have to be careful because if you execute it wrongly, your rival can smash the ball quickly without giving you time to react. Therefore, these types of lobs are usually played by the **opponent's unskilled shoulder**.

For example, if our rival is right-handed, his non-skilled shoulder will be the left one. If we shoot a quick lob that goes over his left shoulder, this opponent will take longer to set up the gesture and our chances of the lob passing him will be higher.

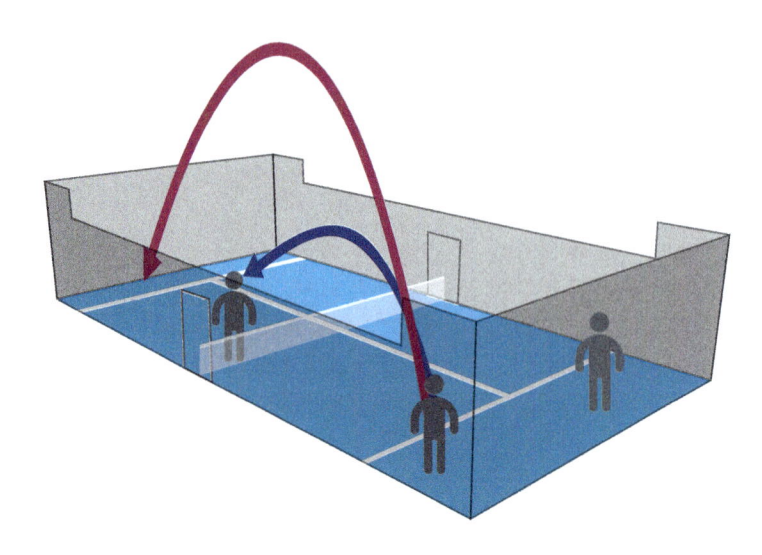

In later sections we will see that these lobs are used in specific situations. Depending on the moment and our intentions, we will have to use one more than the other.

WAYS TO WIN THE NET

Remember that, from the defence zone, our main goal will be to win the net or counterattack. When we win the net, we can set ourselves the goal of winning the point. Ways to win it:

1-TRADITIONAL

The **traditional way to win the net** is to wait for an easy ball to be able to shoot a good lob that ends up overtaking our rivals. Once the rivals turn and let the ball bounce, the players who have thrown the lob will go up to the net.

But at this advanced level, we will have to start practising other methods of winning the net or counterattack mechanisms.

2-CHIQUITA

Chiquita is a shot made by the player who is in the defence zone. It consists of a forehand or backhand shot (it can be played after the wall) **towards the feet of the rivals** who are at the net. Taking into account that the attacking opponents are usually between 2 and 3 metres from the net, our *chiquita* **will generally be a soft ball that will pass a few centimetres above the net**. In this way, we will prevent our rivals from attacking us with power shots, since they will be hitting the ball below the level of the net, forcing them to throw the ball upwards.

Being a shot that requires a certain precision, **we will make a *chiquita* when we have an easy ball**, which means it will be an alternative to the lob. After throwing a *chiquita* we will have different moves to make:

-Once we have thrown a good *chiquita*, we can go up to the net area to cause a volleys battle. Taking advantage of the fact that the rivals will only be able to throw the ball in an upward direction, it is recommended that the defenders, who are going up, make a short break (split) before the opponents hit. This way, they will be able to react better to the next ball that is thrown at them. The most common thing about this move is that it ends in a volleys battle or a shot that surprises the opponent, since the players will be very close to each other and the reaction time will be reduced.

-The *chiquita* also has the function of fixing or attracting the opponents near the net. That is, if we execute a *chiquita*, it is most likely that the attackers will come closer to hit the ball to avoid having to hit the ball from very low. This will allow that, if the defenders who have shot a *chiquita* then throw a lob, they will force the rival to travel greater distance causing the lob to go over them or making a bad *bandeja*.

-It also sets a precedent in the game. If the defenders execute a lob every time they have an easy ball, there comes a time when the attackers anticipate the move, preventing our lobs from overshooting them so often.

On the other hand, if we alternate *chiquitas* and lobs, the rivals will be doubting what move the defender is going to make. That uncertainty always works in favour of the defender, since it has the attacker on edge.

NOTA: If we are in the defence zone and, when playing low, the ball hits the net and passes slowly to our opponent's court, we can take advantage of the fact that they have the ball below the net to counterattack, just as if we had thrown a *chiquita*.

3-STRONG OR LOW BALL + GO UP TO THE VOLLEYS BATTLE

This way of winning the net consists of executing a shot that passes a few centimetres from the net headband and at a certain speed to go up to the net in a volleys battle (since the opponent will not be able to volley down forcefully).

Advanced

By shooting the ball low to the net, we will cause the opponent to only be able to volley deep if he wants to accelerate, or volley at low speed if he wants to play shallow. In this way, going up to the net area, although the rivals are also in it, will not be so complicated. Of course, there are going to be complex reaction situations, quick bounces and fast volleys.

4-GO UP TO BLOCK THE OPPONENT'S *BANDEJA*

This move consists of taking advantage of a good lob thrown by us or a situation where our rival is executing a *bandeja/víbora* shot from an awkward situation to **go up to the net to block his *bandeja* and surprise him**. This move is very common at professional levels. You can even win the net more times this way than in the traditional way.

It consists of cutting down the opponent's time and surprising him. The opponent, when he is executing a *bandeja*, thinks that the defender is going to stay behind waiting for another attempt to win the net again. In this way, if the defender takes advantage of the surprise factor and goes up to the net quickly, blocking the shot, he will later be in an advantageous situation, since the opponent who was shooting the *bandeja* will be far from the net.

This last move has many aspects to highlight and clarify: if we are the attackers, how can we prevent or counteract this move? When to use it? At what point do we have to go up to take advantage of the surprise factor?

If we are the attackers, how can we prevent or counter this move?

If we are the attackers and a rival is going up to block our ball, we have different solutions:

-**Hit the *bandeja* hard** so that the opponent blocks badly.

-Shoot the *bandeja* with a **higher impact height in order to throw the ball vertically towards the feet**. This will cause the opponent to block upwards and we can attack again in case the ball goes in.

-**Change the direction**. If only one of the two players is raising us, we can shoot a *bandeja* to the player who has not gone up to the net. Thus, we will go back to the net and our defenders will be poorly positioned, one at the front and one at the back. If the defender who has fallen behind does not make a very good shot, we can execute our next shot towards the player at the net who will have very little reaction time.

But the most important thing is that we know the opponent is going up to the net zone. For that, we will have to understand that the opponent will make this move when the lob is moderately good to have time to rise. With a short lob, the player will not go up.

If the lob of our defender opponent is good, **our partner has the task of informing us what the rivals are doing**. In the event that the opponent is going up to block the ball, our partner will have to notify us so that we can choose between the options that we have presented previously (hard, at the feet or change of direction). For this, **it is important that our teammate does not look at us as we are shooting the *bandeja*, but instead directs all his attention and his field of vision towards our opponents**.

Your partner, who is reporting on what the opponents are doing, **has to avoid making long sentences or words that could mislead**. Each couple can have their specific ways of talking to each other but mechanising clear words and phrases will allow us to quickly adapt to any partner we have.

Advanced

For example, **using words with one or two syllables** will allow us to give a lot of information at once and to be able to say everything that is happening. If defending opponents are falling behind, saying "back, back, back", "nothing, nothing, nothing", "no, no, no", "drive back" **in a relaxed tone of voice**, it will help your teammate to easily know that he can peacefully shoot a *bandeja*. On the other hand, if we say that "player x is in the defence zone" it may be that while we are saying this long sentence, that player has already gone up to the net and has not given us time to warn our partner.

If it is not expressly mentioned whether it is the forehand or left player who is going forward, it is usually understood that we are referring to the cross-zone player, since our partner's *bandeja* is usually played cross court. But if, for example, we are not throwing the ball to the best player and just throwing it to the worst one, it will be understood that if we do not express anything different we will always be referring to the player to whom we are throwing all the balls.

Therefore, in cases where the opponent's go up late to block the ball, using the "nothing, nothing, nothing" would become "nothing, nothing, **GOING UP**!". If we suddenly change the word and increase the tone of voice, our partner surely understands that something is going to happen and may have time to change the shot or, at least, know that an imminent volleys battle awaits him.

When to use this move? With which lobs is it easier to do? At what point do we have to go up to take better advantage of the surprise factor?

We will use this move when our lob is good and our opponent is shooting the *bandeja* far from the net, in order to have more time to react and go up to the net.

Using the fast lob will prevent us from having time to be able to advance towards the net to block the ball from an advanced zone. On the other hand, by using high lobs we will have time to go up and we can even go up late. This factor will allow us to surprise the opponent causing that, once the partner warns him that we are behind and he relaxes, we can quickly go up to block the ball and surprise him.

THE SECRETS OF PADEL

ADAPTATION TO EXTERNAL FACTORS

A padel match is conditioned by many external factors. The altitude at sea level we are at, the temperature, the type of grass, the wind, the rain, the humidity, the condition of the balls or having the sun facing us will greatly influence the game and the couple who best suits all these factors will win.

At this advanced level, it is important that we have tips to be able to adapt better and win many more games.

Players who have a good smash will use it more when more rebound-friendly factors exist. Instead, they will have to use more *bandejas* or *víboras* in case the ball doesn't bounce as much.

> **The higher the altitude, the more the ball bounces. The higher the temperature, the more the ball bounces. With new balls, the more the ball bounces. With the dry court, the more the ball bounces. If the grass is not so new, the more the ball bounces.**
>
> Some of these factors seem logical. But to what extent are we consistent with them when we play?

Wind

This factor usually causes a lot of problems for both defenders and attackers. It must be clear that the wind affects us, especially when shooting a lob. This sport is played between walls, therefore, when playing low, the wind does not influence so much. The easy alternative for the defenders would be to play shooting fewer lobs, using *chiquitas*, firm balls or low balls going close to the net to get into the game. But we can also try to understand which way the wind is blowing and adapt our game.

Generally the wind tends to go in one direction. There are usually gusts of wind but it is likely that it will always be in the same direction.

If we are defenders and we have the wind in our favour, we will have to be careful with the fast lob, since it is most likely that they will quickly go to the glass.

It is advisable to play high crossed court lobs so the wind makes the ball slip into the opponent's court. We have to watch if the opponent hits a smash correctly, since the wind will accelerate the ball's return to its own court once it hits our wall.

If we are defenders and we have the wind against us, we can use both types of lobs. The fast lob will be very useful because we will be able to throw it at a higher speed, which will cause the rival to not be able to put together a shot quickly. If we use the high lob, it will have to be strong and in the direction of the opponent's court, waiting for the wind to stop the ball. In the event that our opponent makes a smash, the wind will play in our favour since it will slow down the ball on its return after having touched the wall.

If we are attacking with the wind in our favour, the lobs of our opponents will slow down, therefore we will have to anticipate that the lobs that were short will be even shorter and that the good lobs of the opponents will be more comfortable. But be careful with the lobs that you think are going out, they might come in! Therefore, prevention is better than cure. If we are attacking with the wind in our favour, we can play a little further back from the net than when we play without the wind.

In case we make a smash, we have to bear in mind that, once the ball hits the back wall and returns to our court, the ball will lose speed very quickly due to the influence of the wind. In other words, if we attack with the wind in our favour, it is likely that the opponent will leave more short lobs, but let's be careful with the wind when we are going to smash because it will also affect the return of the ball.

If we are attacking against the wind, the lobs of our opponents will go further and further, therefore we will have to anticipate that the lobs that were going to be short will be better than we thought and that the good lobs of the opponents will go straight out. The opponents will hardly throw us fast lobs, since they have the wind in their favour. Therefore, if we are attacking against the wind, we can play a little closer to the net than when we play without the wind.

If we do a smash, we have to keep in mind that once the ball hits the back glass and returns to our court, it will quickly gain speed due to the influence of the wind. In other words, if we attack against the wind, we will probably have problems coordinating the shot, but if we execute it well, the wind will help us return the ball faster.

If the wind is lateral, we will have to adapt the direction of our lob, not its power. If we are the attackers, we will have to think that the point of impact is going to be altered.

In situations of high wind gusts or variable wind direction:

-If you are the attackers, try not to build up the shot too much in order to have a short distance from the point of impact and be able to quickly adapt your movement. Try to score more points with the volley than with the smash.

-If you are the defenders, try to play lower and win the net with *chiquitas* or volleys battle. If not, take advantage of the fact that the opponent will be indecisive with his shots to shoot lobs and take advantage of mistakes.

Rain or humidity

With rain or humidity the balls will weigh more, bounce less, slip more when they touch the racket or the ground and fall when they touch the glass with a descending trajectory.

Therefore, the tips to keep in mind are:

→**If we're defending**, we'll play further back and play flatter shots. We'll get closer to the back wall and closer to the side wall. That way, we'll only let the ball through the back wall if it is too deep or if we see that it will touch the wall on its way up. Side walls will have to be avoided. Anticipating the side wall to hit a straight forehand or backhand can help a lot.

The rival will not be able to score points with the smash, therefore the lobs are not in danger of being won by over the fence or power smash.

→**If we are attackers**, we will avoid playing with too many effects. The ball will slip when it hits the racket, therefore we will use flatter shots. Playing towards the side walls may cause more problems for the opponent than playing towards the fences. We will have to use the *bandeja* more than the smash. Playing strong balls into the box will cause the opponent not to want to let the balls enter the wall for fear of slipping, receiving very heavy and difficult balls. Let's try not to lose the net, since defending will be more difficult. Therefore, if good lobs are thrown at us, an extra effort will have to be made to try to touch the ball shooting a *bandeja* and go up again even if situations of volleys battle occur.

Advanced

Radiant sun and face

Even playing with the sun in your face can be annoying. When we have the sun in our face and it bothers us when looking at the ball, these tips can be of great help:

→See if it only bothers you when the ball comes from the forehand zone or from the backhand zone. That is, sometimes the sun is not right in front and in the centre. It may be that the ball bothers us more when it comes from one direction than from another. Considering whether to play our balls in the area so that the sun does not affect us will make the balls coming from there less complicated.

→If the sun has bothered us a lot when attacking, when we change sides and defend, let's use this factor in our favour. We will shoot more lobs to keep opponents' eyes up longer.

→Another fundamental help is not to focus 100% of our vision on the ball, if it is right in the area of the sun. Slightly looking away and having the ball in the background until there is little time left for impact will allow us to feel less uncomfortable.

USEFUL ACCESSORIES

Using accessories that help us soften these adverse effects will be of great help. Wear sunglasses or hats. Overgrips, wristbands or straps, so that the sweat does not reduce the grip of the handle.

If the sports shoes are in better condition and with an engraved sole (herringbone), it will make it easier for us to adhere to the court.

PERFECTION IN ATTACKING SHOTS

At this advanced level, we will have to perfect moves to seek to win the point more frequently.

→The **topspin to the fence or roller**, is a shot that is made from the attack zone and is characterised by seeking the fence to make it difficult for the opponent to hit the ball. It is a characteristic shot of right-handed players who play in the

THE SECRETS OF PADEL

backhand zone or left-handed players who play in the forehand zone. It is usually used when the opponent's lob is angled and close to the side of the court. Let's recall what was explained in the "Theory of angles" section of the intermediate level.

To make this shot, the highest possible impact height is usually sought to have more angle. If we practice it by giving the ball topspin we can have more control when we master it.

→ The **víbora** is a shot that is characterised by having lateral effect. It is a shot that can be executed more aggressively and quickly than a *bandeja*. Taking into account the "Theory of effects", explained in the intermediate level, in this shot right-handers hit the ball between 3 and 4 o'clock and left-handers between 8 and 9 o'clock.

The impact height is similar to the *bandeja*. The lower the impact height, the more risk of failure, but if it goes in it will bounce less.

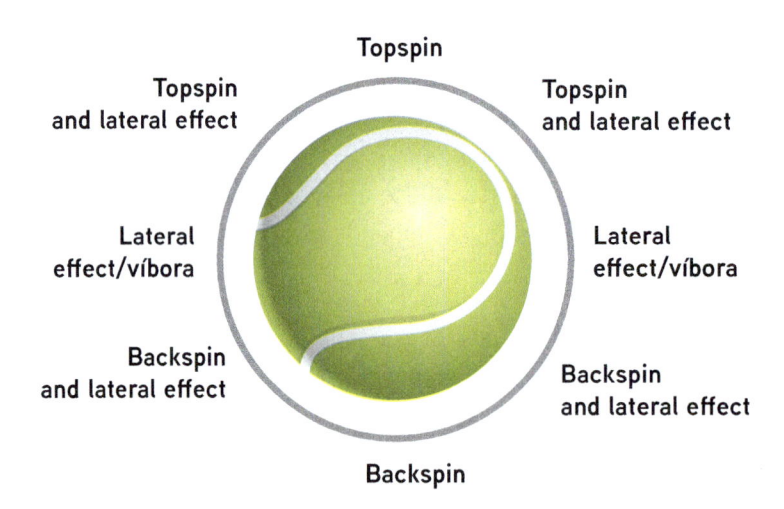

Topspin

Topspin and lateral effect | Topspin and lateral effect

Lateral effect/víbora | Lateral effect/víbora

Backspin and lateral effect | Backspin and lateral effect

Backspin

→ The **backhand volley to the fence** is a characteristic shot of right-handed players who play on the left side of the court or left-handed players who play on the right side. Since the defenders usually play to our backhand volley in order to prevent us from throwing power volleys at them, a widely used variant is to take advantage of the angle we have to play towards the opposite cross fence.

Advanced

→The **smash over fence** is a power shot characterised by having a topspin effect to facilitate the ascence of the rebound of the ball so that it comes off the side of the court. Taking into account the "Theory of effects", explained in the intermediate level, in this shot the right-handers hit the ball between 12 o'clock and half past one. Left-handers between half past ten and 12 o'clock.

→The **forehand or drive volley** has to start to cause difficulties for the opponent in the usual way. We can use it with a lot of backspin for those balls that come close to the height of the net, and try to smash the ball on the ground. Another very effective variant is volley flat with power, or even topspin, those balls that come high.

→The **high ball off the back glass (*bajada*)** that we discussed at the end of the intermediate level can be done in different ways depending on the position of our opponents and depending on how we have left the ball. Remember that in the section "Initiation to the high ball off the back glass" we discussed when to use it and what factors had to be given.

Now, we will clarify whether to play it flat, backspin or *víbora*:

→The **flat *bajada*** can be done with balls that have not been too high. By using a flat shot, we will have more control in the direction and we will be able to make a lot of power. In situations in which the opponent is very close to the net, it will be a very good option to run it this way.

→The ***bajada* with sidespin (*cuchilla*)** has to be made with balls that have remained high. By using a lateral effect, we will make it difficult for our opponent to read the ball. It is a shot that even with the opponent staying in the area of defence can be very useful. Its execution is more complicated.

→The **backspin *bajada*** can also be done with balls that have not been too high. It will be ideal to execute it in situations where both opponents or one of them does not want to go up to the net. The backspin ***bajada*** will be a difficult ball if the delayed opponent let the ball bounce to the back wall and we will be able to recover the net. Many ***bajadas*** usually have some backspin effect, as they are performed from the top downwards. In here, we are referring to those type of ***bajada*** in which the player prioritises the effect to the power.

THE SECRETS OF PADEL

Another way to execute the *bajada* is by throwing the ball towards the fences. These *bajadas* require a lot of precision, since the ball has to go down quickly because we have little distance to the fences. They are usually executed by deceiving the opponents with body movements that hide the moment of impact. Although they are risky shots, if you shoot cross court, you will have more chances of success, since you will have more distance, angle and the opponents will be tilted closing the centre of the court.

READ THE GAME AND ANALYSE THE OPPONENTS WELL

Studying our opponents from the warm-up will allow us to be efficient in our game system or tactics to use.

There are **more basic and obvious aspects**: see if there is a left-handed player in the opposing pair, see how tall they are, see if they warm up or use smash hits or víbora shots or their level of agility, which you can pick up on in the early stages.

Other aspects, such as the percentage of hits or the effectiveness of their shots, will have to be evaluated as the game progresses and the points are added. The more points and exchanges, the more reliable statistics we can obtain and the better conclusions we will achieve.

It is very important that, in order to get a good statistic of the opponent's game, you take into account what was mentioned in the final section of the intermediate level, "The mood factor". Remember that, if the rivals have the score in favour of a score of 40/0, it is most likely that they will play risky and brave shots. Therefore, in your statistics, it is important that you value how your rivals play but also take into account what situation they were in when they executed certain shots.

Apart from studying our rivals to be efficient with our movements, it is important to read the game and each move that is made to be able to guess what balls will be generated and to be able to anticipate or react faster. That is, **play two sight balls or more**.

Basic example

If I'm attacking and our defender is known for throwing a lot of lobs, if I shoot an easy volley for our defender, he'll most likely throw a lob, right? Therefore, if we are aware of this, we will surely react faster when the lob is thrown at us and we will fall back in time.

Advanced example

If we are attacking and my partner gets hit with a good lob, if I see that my opponent stays behind and my partner shoots him a *bandeja*, I can sense that the opponent will try to throw the ball at his feet because he will be going up. Therefore, once my partner shoots the *bandeja* and the opponent is about to hit the ball, I can move slightly to the centre of the court to intercept that volley (taking a positional risk) and thus prevent my partner from being left behind. in a bad situation or cut off my opponents' counterattack.

Sometimes, we can even play with these factors in reverse. If we want to surprise, the most efficient thing will be to accustom the opponents to a certain type of ball so that at key moments we can use the move we want to surprise them and that they do not expect it.

This will be a fundamental aspect at the next level, the professional level.

PROFESSIONAL

After innumerable matches lived, lost, come from behind, won or abandoned, many lessons and trainings carried out, after having played in all existing conditions, having analysed thousands of opponents and having learned a great variety of resources... Some will be able to access the **professional** level.

A level in which we will have a very high precision. Where the emotional factor and mental stability decide the most even matches. Physical fitness is not a feature, but a necessity. **The details make the difference because the basics of the game are taken for granted**.

In this level, we will observe the details and aspects that characterise the players that are in it. Advice that players of lower levels will be able to understand and use but that at this level will make a difference. These details will be very relevant to decide who ends up winning the match, since all the aspects of the game discussed in the previous levels will be carried out perfectly by the four players on the court.

Therefore, all these tips and advice that we are going to comment on and explain can be understood and put into practice by players of **lower levels**. But it may be that putting them into practice leads to increased errors in the game.

SERVICE AND MECHANISE POSSIBLE OPENINGS

In the advanced level, we discussed the importance of analysing all the possibilities that can occur after directing our service to the T zone, the side wall or the body.

The professional player has to analyse:

→ The opponent's previous serve returns stat, seeing what executions he has performed and his result.

→ The current score and moment, since a score for or against will affect the risk, intentions and daring of the opponent and our own.

→ The advantages and disadvantages of where to direct the service, taking into account the strengths and weaknesses of the four players.

Taking these aspects into account, we can imagine or predict what moves we will receive and, therefore, anticipate an attack hit on our part.

At this level, if we miss the first service, the returner will have no difficulty trying to execute a move that allows him to win the net or take away the attacking initiative. We must try to have a very high percentage of success with the first service.

Starting from the idea that when we serve with the first service, the opponent will generally return from the bottom because they will have difficulties, we will try to maintain the pressure with our volleys or we can even execute a direct shot (winner) to shorten the point. But **it will be important that our partner also knows where we will serve** so that he can also foresee the next move. Telling my partner where I am going to serve in a way that the rival does not notice will help us greatly because it reduces the chances that we can find ourselves in doubtful situations later.

THE SECRETS OF PADEL

For example, imagine that we are a right-handed left player. Our partner is also right-handed. If we have to serve with 15/15 (from the right to the left side of the court) with the Australian modality, if we decide to serve towards the side wall, it is highly recommended that we tell our partner so that he covers the centre of the court for us. Because serving with the Australian modality to the side wall, we have a certain risk that our opponent will be able to anticipate the ball and try to throw down the line causing us not to reach the first volley easily.

Once I have communicated to my partner where I am going to serve my first service, we can go up to the net with the intention of:

→ If the opponent returns down the line to our backhand volley, we can try to execute the backhand volley to the opposite cross fence. And, immediately afterwards, quickly tilt to the centre of the court to define with a forehand volley, in case the opposing left player hits the next ball wrong, which is very likely.

→ If the opponent throws the ball towards my forehand volley, if the ball is a little high and slow, I can try to volley flat or topspin with power. If the ball comes lower, I can try to smash or bury the ball. In case I manage to smash the ball, since the opponent will not be able to lob, I will be able to get closer to the net to define the next ball more easily.

→ If the opponent returns the ball cross court, as my partner has already been warned, he will surely be very efficient with the choice of his next shot, which will allow us to have more facilities to continue with the initiative of the shot.

In case we miss the first service, we will have to adopt a more passive and supportive situation. We will try to make a second service towards an area that the opponent cannot counterattack so easily but be very alert because he has many options to generate moves to win the net. Serving towards the body or to the centre of the court allows the point to start with less risk to the passings, since the opponent from the centre of the court has less angle to return the ball to the sides. In addition, we move the opponent, leaving his corner uncovered. On the other hand, by taking out the centre with a second service, our rival will have many facilities to start with a good lob.

DO NOT ABUSE THE GAME PATTERN

High level matches often have game tendencies and tactics that are repeated for almost the entire match. Rivals find a game system or game pattern that allows them to play more comfortably, either by generating points or not suffering in defence.

The problem may be that, if a couple abuses carrying out these tactics and mechanisms all the time, there comes a time when the opponents find a solution or adjust to it and they turn the game around.

That is why it is important to assess the tactics that are used and see if the match needs to use those mechanisms at certain times or at all times.

Basic example

If the opponents pair is made up of a tall player who hits the smash very well and a short player who does not finish well, we will have to see if shooting the lob all the time to the short one works. Different factors may alter the course of the match:

→It may be that at the beginning of the match the balls are new and all the smashes of the tall player are winners. But it may happen that the smashes become less effective due to the deterioration of the balls as the sets progress, that suddenly the temperature drops as it gets dark, that it rains, that this player has doubts or has the sun in his face...

→It may happen that the short player does not shoot well but we do not find a way to win the net either. By throwing the lob at him all the time, it may be that he varies his **bandejas** or **bajadas** and ends up doing us more damage.

→At key moments, it may happen that this opponent pair anticipates our movements because we are doing the same thing all the time. It is possible that the tall player intuits and anticipates our lob and ends up smashing anyway from his partner's area.

Advanced example

Let's imagine that the two components of the opponents pair (who are left-handed and right-handed) have a similar level but we feel more comfortable throwing the lob to the right-handed player (playing on the left side of the court) since their *bandejas* are easy to defend by our player on the left side of the court. If from the first games we use this tactic and we even get ahead on the scoreboard, it may happen that the opponent pair detects our tactic and looks for solutions:

→It could be that the left-handed player takes more court and ends up playing it.

→It may be that the right-handed player varies the direction of his *bandejas* and ends up bothering more.

→It could be that the right-handed player ends up playing differently, being more aggressive or looking for more balls to the lateral zone to make it difficult for our defending player.

So we see that the opponents pair can find solutions to easily turn the score and the game around. It would be optimal that, if the game is even and we have a light tactic that allows us to play more comfortably, we use it when we need it. If from the fifth minute of the game we always do the same thing, it is very likely that the tactic will lose effectiveness.

But what if we use this tactic when the score is 30/30 or 30/40? Of course we are not saying that the other points have no value and we play randomly. But if we have other options that make the game remain even, waiting for the right moment to propose the game system we want can mean that we are more effective and that even the opponent does not realise so quickly the game pattern that we are proposing.

PLAY WITH THE SCOREBOARD AND HAVE ACES UP YOUR SLEEVE

As we discussed in the previous section, it is important that at key moments we use mechanisms or moves that allow us to play more comfortably or that can surprise the opponent without having to risk too much.

Therefore, it is very important to have mechanised moves so that they are effective when we use them and wait for the right moment to carry them out.

Professional

For example, let's imagine a very even match where I get my opponent used to defending by staying behind and I don't volley or go up to block his *bandejas*. Thus, when this opponent is in the net, he will attack calmly.

If after many games playing like this, we find ourselves with a score of 4/4 and a break ball, if I throw a good lob and go up to block his *bandeja*, I will surely surprise him and my move will be very effective. That's because my opponent had not received this move in any of the previous games and was not expecting this. In this way, the move of going up and blocking his *bandeja* gains effectiveness as the surprise factor is huge. Maybe we can get the break ball and score 5/4 and service. The opponent has little room for manoeuvre to react, since if we make the next game we will close the set.

If we have already made this same move several times in previous games, it is very likely that our opponent will expect it and we will lose effectiveness when making it again.

These moves, if used at key and opportune moments, can be considered as aces up a player's sleeve. The best players can play in a linear way if they have control

THE SECRETS OF PADEL

of the match, but if the match is even and the turning points arrive, these players will change or vary some moves to surprise their opponents and decline the match in their favour. Therefore, it is important to have these moves well trained so that they are not risky to execute.

Some of these moves have already been discussed as variants in previous chapters:

→ Go up to block the opponent's *bandeja*.

→ Change the direction in which we usually throw the *bajada de pared*.

→ In the volley zone, entering our partner's zone and anticipating the ball.

→ Going from throwing fast lobs to very high lobs.

→ Throw *chiquitas* with the easy balls and go up to the volleys battle.

→ Any change to the game structure that is different from what was being used.

GO UP LATE TO BLOCK OR BACK DOWN

A nuance of this level is that the moves can be more effective if they are made just at the exact moment in which the opponent cannot vary his shot. This moment is usually a little late and implies that we do it quickly.

If we shoot a high lob and instantly run up to block the opponent's *bandeja*, it is very likely that this opponent will notice or his teammate will warn him and end up varying his shot. This would decrease the effectiveness of the move.

It would be optimal to wait a moment before going up to the net to block his *bandeja*. Waiting for our opponent to relax and even for his partner to have told him that there is no one in the net zone to raise quickly, causing confusion and surprise. We will gain a lot of effectiveness in the move and we will even generate doubts in the later moves, since our opponent will be watching us all the time and his indecisions will increase.

The same thing can happen if we intentionally do it the other way around. That is, if immediately after shooting a high lob we go up to the net causing our opponent to see us or his teammate to warn him and then we back down quickly before he shoots the *bandeja*, we are likely to receive a different ball that will allow us to counter-attack. It is very likely that our opponent will hit hard from top to bottom thinking that we will receive the ball quickly at our feet, but having backed down, we will have a ball with an ideal rebound to take the initiative.

SHOT PREPARATIONS THAT CAUSE THE OPPONENTS TO HESITATE

We are at a level where the details make the difference. And there is no better way to do it other with our body position, body expression and shot preparation can start to cause uncertainty and deceive our opponents.

For this, the easiest thing will be that from the same preparations or armed movements we can execute several different shots. It will also be ideal that our shots preparations allow us to be able to choose to execute them with more or less force.

In the defence zone, having short preparations close to the impact zone of a forehand or a backhand shot will allow us to choose to play low or throw a lob at the last moment. This will make our opponent on edge. For this, it is also important that the height of the racket preparation does not condition our shot.

If we prepare the racket above the ball, executing a lob will be more complicated because we will have to lower the racket to raise it again to throw the lob. Therefore, it is better that in the defence zone we have low and short preparations.

Opening the hand or closing it in the preparation of the shot can also greatly deceive our opponent. For example, if we open our hand in a defensive forehand shot (we open the face of the racket) our opponent will surely think that we will execute a lob, although we can use this gesture to deceive the opponent and end up executing a topspin shot from below so that the ball reaches his feet.

On the contrary, if we put together a ground drive shot with the tightest hand, surely our opponent senses that we will play low. But if at the last moment we open the face of the racket and execute a rising shot, we can overcome our opponent with a lob.

THE SECRETS OF PADEL

We must be careful about altering or modifying preparations as this will surely make our level of control or precision over the shot decrease. That is why it is important to train it and, above all, to do it with shots and gestures that can have fairly homogeneous preparations.

In the zone in the shots of the left players, it is very important to have a preparation that causes doubts in the opponent about whether I am going to execute a smash or a topspin to the fence (**rulo**).

Body expression plays a very important role. If we have our arm and our elbow raised up well prepared and our legs are under tension and flexed, the opponent will surely perceive that we are going to execute a power shot. This can cause that before we shoot it, it goes ahead thinking that the ball is going to bounce a lot. If we then decide to execute another variant of the shot, either to the fence or a *víbora*, the player is likely to be in a worse place.

Even our footstep sounds and intensity can help. If we are a left player who sometimes executes the smash, if after a lob from our opponents towards our partner, we shout loudly "Mine! Mine! Mine!, if we move quickly and energetically towards the striking zone where the lob is going to bounce, our opponents will most likely think that we are going to perform another smash.

Then, we can use that deception or "theatre" to put together a smash shot, causing our opponents to start running towards the net to return the ball after the big bounce that is going to be, but we will end up feinting and executing a soft and shallow hit that will not reach the back wall.

EXCELLENCE IN THE SMASHES AND ITS VARIANTS

→The **smash over the fence** is ideal if your preparation is identical to when we shoot a topsin to the fence.

On courts where there is outside play, this preparation will cause the opponent to leave the door late. Another important nuance for it to be a perfect shot is that the ball comes out of the court between the focus area and the 4-metre side fence. That will make the ball come out very openly and that the opponent, even if he is off the court, will have to go back and will not finish by throwing the ball into the net or hitting hard.

→The **topspin to the fence** (*rulo*) is ideal if its preparation is identical to the smash over the fence. In addition, there are variants such as the so-called backspin smash to the fence, a shot in which right-handers shoot the ball in the area between 2

THE SECRETS OF PADEL

o'clock and 3 o'clock. This increases the probability that the fence will be more irregular and, in cases where the ball deviates at the beginning of the side wall, with this effect, when it reaches the back wall it will hardly bounc..

→The **right-to-right smash** is the smash that a right-handed player makes when he wants to direct his smash from the right zone to the left zone. Right-handers usually take the ball out over the fence by the right zone of the court, since as they will usually shoot the ball through its right hemisphere, the effect they generate always goes to the right once the ball touches the back wall.

In this type of smash, if the right-handed player wants to shoot the ball from the opposite side, that is, from the left side of the court, he will have to use a lot of inertia in the direction of his shot. In addition, some very skilled right-handed players manage to rotate their wrist to the left at the moment of impact, managing to touch the ball in the 11 o'clock area. Thus, the ball takes a left-handed effect and causes the ball to go to the left when it touches the back wall.

In the case of **lefties**, it will be the opposite case. The normal thing is that their smash over the fence is executed at the left zone of the court. Therefore, if they want to hit the ball from the right lateral area, they will have to try to take an angle so that the ball gets inertia to the right when they direct the ball towards the back wall of this zone. If they are able to rotate their wrist to the right when they hit the ball, they will be able to touch the ball at 1 o'clock, achieving an effect that will make the ball go to the right zone once it hits the back wall.

→The **power smash** is the smash with which the speed and aggressiveness of the hit are prioritised. It is usually used flat and parallel so that the ball returns to our field as soon as possible. As it does not have a topspin effect, it is highly recommended that we try to bounce the ball not very deep, so that it can touch the back wall in its highest area and we manage to lift the ball a lot so that it reaches our side without the opponent being able to reach the ball.

On other occasions, this smash can be used without looking for height and simply making the point due to the violence of its hit, causing a very fast ball that does not give the opponent time to react.

→The **smash in suspension** is characterised by its spectacularity in the execution. It requires a previous jump that allows the player to gain impact height to be able to lift the ball more. It can be done with spin or completely flat depending on your intention. Perhaps it is the most difficult smash, since it takes great coordination and body strength to make it perfect.

→The **feint of the smash (fake smash)** is a shot that will create doubts in the opponents and will sometimes help to win the point more easily without having to get to the smash. For a player to feint well, it is necessary that the opponent believes him. That is to say, if he usually smashes, he will be able to feint them later. In addition, he will have to use many body gestures and large preparations that deceive the opponents. It can be used as a variant to any type of smash mentioned. The longer we take to stop the execution to make the soft hit that is required, the more we will deceive our opponents.

The previous smash directions chosen will cause the opponents to move in a certain way. Therefore, where to throw the feint will be very important.

First example

A right-handed player playing in the left zone who throws smashes over the fence all the time on the right side of the court, can cause his opponents to position themselves in the following way:

→The opponent left side player will run around the fence, avoiding chances of being hit by the smash and also being closer to the door.

→The opponent right side player will surely position himself in the T zone or even close to his partner's zone, so that if the expected smash over the fence is executed, he can help his partner to return the ball after the fence, in case of that there are doubts about whether the ball comes out or not.

This would allow us to feint more effectively in parallel. Directing the fake smash near the left side of the court.

Second example

A right-handed player playing in the left zone who, from the centre of the court, uses both the smash over the fence in the right zone and in the left zone, can cause his opponents to position themselves in the following way:

→The opponent left side player will run around the fence, avoiding chances of being hit by the smash and also being closer to the door.

→The opponent right side player will likely do the same as his partner. He will run down the left side zone.

This would allow us to feint more effectively in the centre, since we will have both opponents at the ends of the court.

It also depends a lot on where the lob was thrown at us.

Third example

If we are a right-handed player playing in the right zone and we usually throw the smash over the fence in parallel so that it comes out on the right side of the court:

→If the player in front of us has thrown us a lob from the T zone, it is likely that when we put together the smash, this opponent will run down the centre of the court, which would allow us to feint on the right side area.

NOTE: Opponents may not position themselves exactly like this. There are couples in which the same player always runs forward and stays to cover the possible threat himself.

→If the player in front of us has thrown us a lob from the lateral area (corner), it is likely that when we put together the smash, this opponent will run through the area near the fence, which would allow us to feint on the central right area of the court.

→The **flat power *bandeja*** is a *bandeja* that tries to surprise the opponent with its speed. Since the *bandeja* is usually shot with backspin effect to cause little rebound, this variant tries to hit the ball flat, at high speed and bounce deep so that it comes out with a lot of rebounce.

Normally, it is usually played in the centre of the court to cause the opponents to be more hesitant about who has to run to return the ball. Depending on the height of impact caught and the depth of the bounce that we choose, the ball will come out higher or lower.

Some right-handed drive players also throw it cross court so that the ball reaches the fence at high speed after touching the back wall.

CUTTING THE OPPONENTS' TIME IS NECESSARY

In some sections of previous levels we have commented on the importance of **modifying our positions or anticipating** hits to cause the opponents to have less reaction time to return the next ball.

At this level, playing linear and waiting for opponents to lose the net is often unsuccessful.

Generating different moves such as volleys battle, blocking the opponent's *bandeja*, shooting *chiquitas* and advancing our positions, playing low to the net headband and going up, become common ways of winning the net. In extreme cases when the opponents smash from any position. These moves will be the options that will allow us to win the net the most.

Waiting for an easy ball to throw a lob may no longer be such a good option. There will be games in which the high level of smash of the opponents makes the lob thrown from the back of the court very unproductive and even unfeasible. But perhaps, **if we advance our defensive positions and throw volley lobs or half volley lobs**, we will cause the opponents to not have time to set up their shots or to do so poorly. It is clear that the level of difficulty of making these moves is very high, therefore, training them will be essential.

In attack, we will try to give our defending opponents as little time as possible to think. Therefore, it will generally be better to direct balls **that bounce into the service box** and **force the opponents to play without the wall**. Not playing deep will prevent our opponents from using the wall to give them more time to react or think about how to counterattack.

If we execute fast volleys or *bandejas* with a backspin effect towards the opponent's service box, it will force our opponents to use direct hits or difficult half volleys, which will allow us to generate imprecise returns that we can take advantage of to finish the point.

IRON MENTALITY. ANALYSE EVERYTHING THAT HAPPENS AROUND US

Everything matters and everything influences the game. A great professional player will be aware of everything that happens. Both the errors, the successes and the mood of oneself, the partner or the opponents, as well as the constant state of the balls or the variation of the weather.

Our brain has to constantly analyse everything and draw conclusions. Knowing if our opponent is in a state of grace or if he is usually making the same move on us. Knowing how to stop the pace of the game if our partner is tired. See that the ball has deteriorated or that the temperature has dropped and the smashes are becoming less effective. Detect game patterns that are being repeated to counteract or take advantage of them.

A padel match can change at times. Having the game controlled one hundred percent is impossible. Therefore, if we are winning, we cannot relax or lower our guard at any time. An unexpected error or a ball touching the net passing to the other side can cause the opponents to have a breakpoint at any time, increasing their confidence and our doubts.

In the same way that we should never throw in the towel. We have to trust that the state of grace and confidence of our opponents can be twisted at any time. Coming back from games is easier than it seems, the desire and positive attitude have to prevail at all times, until the last point. Even once we've lost the match, we can't let anger or impotence make us believe that we're worse than we are or that we're out of luck.

Tranquillity, positivism and reflection after the defeat. Not sinking is the only way to be able to try again with our best abilities and win to the fullest. You must analyse the entire game and all the moves that have been made. Even analyse the moment before the match: the physical state in which you were, the stress, the concentration, the warm-up carried out and your attitude. Only then will you be able to draw productive tactical or technical conclusions.

After the victory, you must make self-criticism of the bad moments (if there have been any) to try to improve. Let tranquillity prevail over excess euphoria, because when we lose, the defeat will be worse to accept. Let us value what we have done well and enjoy it. Let's not think that our virtues or genius are something normal. Let's enjoy the moment and the victory, but let's relativize and continue working to improve.